J. E. MOREN

THE CLASSIC CHRISTIAN FAITH

To the students of Gustavus Adolphus College
who have provided the occasion and the inspiration
for this attempt to confess the classic Christian faith
in the language of our world and time.

The
Classic
Christian Faith

Chapel Meditations
Based on
Luther's Small Catechism

By
Edgar M. Carlson

AUGUSTANA PRESS   ROCK ISLAND, ILL.

THE CLASSIC CHRISTIAN FAITH

Library of Congress Catalog Card Number 59-9093

⟦ PRINTED
IN U·S·A ⟧

AUGUSTANA BOOK CONCERN
Printers and Binders
ROCK ISLAND, ILLINOIS
1959

Foreword

SOME TRIPS ARE MEMORABLE because of their destinations; others, because of experiences along the way. A recent trip from Minneapolis to Chicago was put into the latter category by my reading the manuscript of *The Classic Christian Faith.*

When Dr. Edgar Carlson asked me if I would write a foreword, he stated that the publication of these chapel talks might have value on the ground that "they are perhaps typical of college chapel talks"; hence, he inferred, they would reveal to the reader something of the spirit of the Christian college. Candor compels me to say they are not typical; this is very much to their credit, and it is also evidence of what actually can be done at a Christian college.

If less significant chapel talks have profoundly affected the lives of generations of college students, as I am confident they have, how much more can be expected from such talks as these! But it is important to note that such a series of talks could be heard with regularity only on the campus of a Christian college.

Let us dispose once and for all of the notion that daily chapel or courses in Christianity—or the two together—constitute the distinguishing marks of the Christian college, for they do not. The truly distinguishing characteristic of the Christian college is a powerfully motivating desire on the part of the entire college community—the focus being in the administration and faculty—that religion should have the free run of the campus. The central importance of religion is acknowledged, and the search for truth in every department is governed by the primary belief that Christ the Creator is Truth; and furthermore that knowledge of the creation is ultimately meaningful only when related to the Creator.

It was out of such a matrix that these talks emerged. Gustavus Adolphus College is not a Christian college because these chapel talks were given; to the contrary, the talks were given because Gustavus is a Christian college.

Dr. Carlson is a theologian who simplifies without saying so; he never stoops, never popularizes in the bad sense. It is clear that he is talking to college students whose intelligence he respects. The discourses are the familiar, disciplined talk of an able teacher. There are no great climaxes, yet there is never a feeling of fragmentation. Colossal truths are presented without rhetoric; the talks testify to the power of deep conviction and, as one reads, deep answers to deep. Although Dr. Carlson is a philosopher, philosophy never obtrudes.

These excellent little chapel talks bring the Commandments and the Apostles' Creed alive. Dr. Carlson shows their dynamic relevance to our society, as well as to our personal lives. After reading this book, one can never again think them dusty survivals of another age.

There is no question but that secularism is choking out religion in many segments of our society, including some college campuses; it is apparent from what we read and see that a good many sophisticates classify our culture as post-Christian. Hence there never was a time when clarity and conviction in the expression of Christian truth was more important.

Higher education in America is of critical importance to the strength, welfare, and security of our nation and the world. One of the great elements of strength in our system is its diversity—institutions that are state supported and privately supported, large and small, secular and religious. This volume is a testimonial to the latter. Our church and country would be infinitely poorer, if we did not have colleges where such chapel talks as these are presented as unspectacular daily parts of the life of a worshiping community at study.

Robert Mortvedt
Executive Director,
Board of Christian Higher Education,
Augustana Lutheran Church

Contents

PAGE

Introduction 9

PART I
THE TEN COMMANDMENTS

A Preliminary Question 13
The First Commandment 16
The Second Commandment 20
The Third Commandment 23
The Second Table of the Law 27
The Fourth Commandment 30
The Fifth Commandment 33
The Sixth Commandment 36
The Seventh Commandment 39
The Eighth Commandment 42
The Ninth and Tenth Commandments 45

PART II
THE APOSTLES' CREED

I Believe 51
In God, the Father Almighty 54
The Father Almighty, Maker of Heaven and Earth . . . 57
I Believe in Jesus Christ 60
His Only Son 63
Our Lord 67
Who Was Conceived by the Holy Ghost, Born of the
  Virgin Mary 71
Suffered Under Pontius Pilate 74
Was Crucified, Dead, and Buried 78
Descended into Hell 82

	PAGE
The Third Day He Rose Again from the Dead	86
He Ascended into Heaven	90
And Sitteth at the Right Hand of God the Father Almighty	94
From Thence He Shall Come to Judge the Quick and the Dead	97
I Believe in the Holy Ghost	101
The Holy Christian Church, the Communion of Saints . .	106
The Forgiveness of Sins	110
The Resurrection of the Body	114
The Life Everlasting	118

PART III

THE LORD'S PRAYER

Our Father Who Art in Heaven	124
Hallowed Be Thy Name	128
Thy Kingdom Come	132
Thy Will Be Done, on Earth As It Is in Heaven . . .	136
Give Us This Day Our Daily Bread	140
Forgive Us Our Trespasses, As We Forgive Those Who Trespass Against Us	144
Lead Us Not into Temptation; But Deliver Us from Evil .	148
For Thine Is the Kingdom, and the Power, and the Glory, For Ever and Ever	152
Amen	156

PARTS IV AND V

THE SACRAMENTS

By Grace Are You Saved	161
Holy Baptism	164
The Lord's Supper	168

Introduction

THE BRIEF MESSAGES contained in this volume have all been delivered as chapel talks to the students of Gustavus Adolphus College. Their publication is prompted by a number of requests from generous people, some of whom have expressed the desire for the opportunity to review their contents more thoughtfully than is possible during an oral presentation. However, since they have been delivered over a rather wide span of years, and since such requests have scarcely been of sufficient magnitude to warrant an offering to the general public, some further justification for their printing has been needed.

The church bears an important witness to its great gospel through its institutions of Christian higher education. Every aspect of church college life bears the mark of the Christian dedication by which it is motivated and governed. The central fact by which the church college is distinguished from other institutions of learning is that within it the Word of God is given free course. It is seriously studied as a part of the college curriculum. A basic consideration in the selection of staff members, along with high competence in the field of instruction, is the willingness and desire to be a part of the Christian witness in higher education. Worship services are a regular part of the program of learning and living.

The membership of the church generally has little opportunity to feel the pulse of this Christian witness. It is confronted by reports, statistics, appeals for funds, and an occasional rumor about this or that. Perhaps such a collection of chapel talks as this, constituting a living segment of the worship life that has been experienced at one of the colleges of

9

the church, will be of help in interpreting the real work of Christian higher education. This is at least a hope which their author entertains.

There is a second possible justification for this publication. Over the course of more than a dozen years the author has found it desirable to use the various portions of Luther's *Small Catechism* as a basis for meditations. They do not constitute a single series delivered consecutively during any one year, but usually they have constituted series for a longer or shorter period of time. It is probably eight or ten years ago since the series on the Lord's Prayer was given. Put together in the present form, it could be that they would be useful in connection with adult instruction classes, youth groups, mid-week services, or evening vespers. Perhaps what the author has been led to see and say about this classic summary of the Christian faith will evoke other insights in those who are called upon to interpret the faith to their congregations. We ought not to be through with the *Small Catechism* when the confirmation examination has been passed. It is too important a compendium of the Christian faith for that.

If these should prove to be too ambitious hopes for this little volume, then it will have to be enough that the author has been enriched again by preparing these brief meditations for publication, and that their appearance in print will save him from the temptation of using them again—because someone may have read them.

E. M. C.

PART ONE

The
Ten Commandments

A PRELIMINARY QUESTION

TEXT: *Mark 2:1-12*

THERE ARE A NUMBER OF THINGS about this story concerning Jesus' healing of the man sick of the palsy which might well engage our thought for a few moments, but I have one particular observation which I would like to make. It is perfectly clear from the story that the contemporaries of Jesus took offense at His declaration to the sick man that his sins were forgiven. They regarded this as something far more serious and presumptuous than the claim that He could heal a man, or even that He could raise a man from the dead. When He said to the man sick of the palsy, "Rise, take up your pallet and walk," they did not say, "Who can make men walk except God?" Even when He raised men from the dead, they did not charge Him with blasphemy. Presumably there were other ways of accounting for that than the clear assertion of divinity. But when He said to the sick of the palsy, "My son, your sins are forgiven," they said, "It is blasphemy! Who can forgive sins but God alone?"

If Jesus should have been talking to a twentieth-century crowd on the streets of a modern city, it might very well be that they would have brought their sick to Him now as then. We are not less concerned about the illnesses we cannot cure, despite all that we have learned about sickness and healing since that day. Faith healers are not unheard of, and wherever

13

they appear the hopeful are certain to gather about them.

But if under such circumstances in a contemporary crowd, Jesus had said, "Your sins are forgiven you," would there be any great excitement about it? There might very well be some who would question His authority to do so, but they would probably turn away and go about their business as usual. Would anyone consider that He was offering too much, going beyond anything that He had a right to give? I think, rather, there would be a sigh of disappointment. Is this all there is to the preacher? There is nothing unusual or exceptional about Him after all, then! Who cannot forgive sins?

What I am afraid has happened to the modern world is that it isn't worried very much about being forgiven. It is worrying tremendously about being healed and staying well. Anyone who has anything to offer that will enable men more quickly and more certainly to get up out of bed and walk can have anything that he asks for. And Jesus would not begrudge him, for He was concerned about that, too. But forgiveness, that has become a sort of bagatelle, a trinket that can be picked up anywhere, so universally available that it is hardly worth having.

It may seem to be in contradiction to what I have been saying that our generation is very much aware of "guilt-feelings," but this may really be another way of ignoring the fact of guilt. When we reduce the fact of guilt to a feeling of guilt, and devise ways of getting rid of the feeling without dealing with the fact, we are treating guilt as though it were only an illusion.

If you want to start an argument about Jesus today, you are not likely to get it by saying that Jesus forgives sin. You are far more likely to get it if you say that Jesus heals men; perhaps most likely if you say that He arose from the dead and that He raises others from the dead.

There have been times when the full meaning of the gospel has been communicated to men in that single word "forgiveness," and when the boundary line between the believers and the unbelievers was clearly marked by whether or not men believed that Jesus could forgive their sins. It was so in the days of Jesus and of Paul. It became so again in the Reformation and at intervals since that time. In a real sense it is always true, and always some men have known that it is true, but the message of forgiveness cannot communicate the true meaning of the gospel to us unless we are capable of understanding what divine forgiveness means.

The point which I want to make is that the reason forgiveness has become unimportant for so many of us in the modern world is that *law* has lost its meaning for us. Of course, we use the term and we mean something by it, but it is not the meaning which it has had in those periods of Christian history when men have responded greatly and genuinely to the gospel of forgiveness. We know law as a description of that which happens with such regularity that any deviation from it is not to be expected, as when we speak of the "laws of nature." We know law as a statement of the ideal, of what ought to be. We know law as the rules and regulations which men impose upon themselves through democratic procedures. The Law of God is something other than any or all of these.

"My son, your sins are forgiven," will neither be blasphemous nor redeeming until we face a law which makes us guilty.

THE FIRST COMMANDMENT

TEXT: *Exodus 20:1-6*
"You shall have no other gods before me."

FROM AMONG ALL THE COMMANDMENTS which are recorded in the books to which the Jewish believers gave the title "The Law," there are ten that stand out as entitled to the designation "The Ten Commandments." Although many centuries have passed since they were given specific formulation, and although the enactment of laws has gone on apace during almost every day that has passed, they continue to enjoy that unique place among the laws of many lands and peoples and races which permits them to continue to claim the distinction of *The* Ten Commandments. No one with any serious concern for society would argue for their repeal today, not even the secular and avowedly atheistic nations would dispense with the second table defining the obligations of men within society.

There are plenty of people who think an exception can be made in their case, but no one would seriously argue that all men should steal, kill, commit adultery, show disrespect to parents and to those in authority, or seek for themselves that which belongs to another. No one seriously believes that this would be a better world, if more people disregarded these Commandments. We may yield to the temptation of believing that there would be some personal advantage if we were

16

to step outside the Ten Commandments at some point, but we cannot will that everyone would do so. It was said of the French Revolution that men were taking the "not" out of the Commandments and putting it into the Creed. To whatever extent that was true, it was doomed to failure.

Why is it that these particular Commandments continue to claim authority after these many centuries and in spite of the changes in moral and religious climate from one generation to another? Surely, it is not because they were enunciated by Moses. If we look at the record, it is evident that they were recognized as binding upon men before the time of Moses. He may have codified and collected them, even given them their concrete form, but he did not originate them. They became a part of the basic law and covenant of a people under his initiative and direction, but their authority is neither enhanced by nor dependent upon any part which he had to play in the founding of the Israelitic nation.

We say about these Ten Commandments that they are the "Law of God." By this we mean that they are written into the very structure of the world which He created. They define obligations that are inherent in being His creatures. It may be possible to conceive of a world which would run equally well without respect for life or property or purity or reputation, but it is not this world. The Ten Commandments define the obligation which is laid upon us by the very fact that we exist as persons in this kind of world. They define the obligations which we must assume if we are to be or become persons. We shall have adequate occasion to illustrate this as we move through these Commandments.

What I have been saying may seem to have validity with regard to the Fifth, Sixth, and Seventh Commandments, but does it really have anything to do with the First? "I am the Lord your God, . . . you shall have no other gods before me."

Here, at the outset, we are reminded that our relation to

the Law is also a relation to a Law-Giver. It is not a matter of being convinced that "honesty is the best policy" or that "virtue is its own reward." It is not the definition of what the prudent man would do, if he were clever enough to see all the factors in the situation. The first step, and the crucial one, in recognizing the elemental obligation which is involved in being a person, is that one shall know that he is a creature and therefore under obligation to a Creator—a Creator who does not act capriciously, or temperamentally, or erratically, but who acts consistently according to the law which He has established.

Who are the rival gods whom we may enthrone above Him? It is not likely that any of us shall make graven images and worship them. We may, to be sure, worship wealth, or beauty, or power, or pleasure, and let them become the decisive considerations in everything that we do. But I think the real rival to the throne room which belongs to God is not any of these things which we seek for ourselves, or by which we seek to extend our control over the world. The real rival of God is our *self*. If we attempt to fashion out of this world an empire for ourselves, instead of seeing our lives as a part of a kingdom that is beyond us, nothing that we do can be really right. Self-centeredness will corrupt every virtue, it will pervert every good intent, it will set us over against God whose will is the law of our lives and of the universe about us.

This carries with it an implication, too. I have said that forgiveness of sins seems a little thing to modern man, and that he cannot really understand the gospel of forgiveness unless he understands the law of God. A part of this inability to understand the law lies just here: he who violates the law has not just violated a rule or regulation in a book, a statute— he has set himself against the Law-Giver. He has done violence to the person of God. He has made himself guilty not before a set of words, but before God from whom he has his life and who has determined the conditions under which it may be retained. Our problem is not primarily to adjust ourselves to a situation by conforming to accepted standards, but to be reconciled to a Person who is the source of our being. One can adjust himself to a situation, but he cannot reconcile himself to God. Only God's forgiveness can do that.

THE SECOND COMMANDMENT

TEXT: *Exodus 20:7*
"You shall not take the name of the Lord your God in vain."

IF YOU WERE TO ASK a typical modern American to rate the Ten Commandments on the basis of their importance or value, it is not likely that he would put this one second; it is more likely that he would put it close to the bottom. The careless, thoughtless, and profane use of the divine Name surely seems to the modern man to be a matter of no great consequence, at least if one may reach any conclusion from the frequency with which the Lord's name is taken in vain. But in that collection of laws which we still call The Ten Commandments, it does come second.

We are here dealing with a religious ethic, an ethic in which the First Commandment is that we shall believe, fear, love, and trust God above all else. If that is the First Commandment, then this is the Second. If the fundamental obligation which existence lays upon us is to acknowledge that we are creatures of God, upon whom we are dependent and to whom we are answerable, then the most direct implication of this is that we shall not take His name in vain.

Let us explore a couple of connections between these Commandments. (1) Your name is your most personal and private possession. There may be others who carry a name spelled like yours and pronounced like yours, but no one carries your name. It may have been given to you by someone else, but what it means now is what you have made it mean. It identifies you and no one else. How people react to your name is how they react to you. If you pass a crowd of students and hear your name mentioned, and a titter runs through the crowd, will you comfort yourself with the thought that it was just your name, not you? If the sovereign God passes by, and hears His name used in jest or in anger, is He apt to smile magnanimously and say, "It was just my name, not me"? Surely one of the tests of whether God has any place in our lives is how we handle His name. We cannot argue that what we do with God's name is a little thing, except on the premise that it doesn't matter much what we do with God himself.

(2) A second connection with the First Commandment has to do with the matter of honesty. I remember being somewhat disturbed as a young student when I read somewhere that it was a shortcoming of the Ten Commandments that there was no commandment against lying. I have become convinced that in this instance, as in so many others, the limitations of Scripture, and of the ancient mind in general for that matter, are not due so much to the limitations of the ancients as to the woodenness and lack of imagination in the modern interpreter. The Jews understood this prohibition against taking the name of the Lord in vain as a clear prohibition against dishonesty. Remember how Jesus says, "You have heard that it was said to the men of old, You shall not swear falsely. . . . But I say to you, Do not swear at all. . . . Let what you say be simply 'Yes' or 'No.'" One might put it this way: God would have us treasure our names as He treasures His. Let your name be such that your Yes and No will be enough. Then it will not be necessary to call God to witness in order to assure men of the truth which you assert.

There are, I think, only two possible explanations of the use of profanity. One is that the user is habitually dishonest. He knows that his word cannot be trusted. People know better than to believe him when he speaks in his own name. If he is to expect others to have faith in what he says, he must call in the authority of another higher than himself. I think I could grant a certain validity to this position. If a man is a chronic liar and is willing to have the fact known and proclaimed, it may be necessary for him to support himself by oath in an emergency in which it is exceedingly important that people believe the truth which he has to tell. But, of course, this doesn't excuse him for being that kind of person or having that kind of name. But let him be sure, then, that it is the truth; if he should seek to use the authority of God's name to make his lying and deception successful, be sure the Lord will not hold him guiltless.

The other possible explanation for taking the name of the Lord in vain is that one is habitually profane; it is to admit that one has become so callous to a name which identifies God as one's own name identifies oneself, so callous to a name which represents to us Him who created us, who lived, and loved, and died, and rose again in the person of Jesus Christ, and before whom we shall all some day stand with the judgment of eternity upon us in His hand that we can let that name pass our lips without even its registering in our minds. We can become so blind and deaf to all its high and holy associations that it becomes only an exclamation point in our speech. What a horrible state to come to! I would personally much rather admit to being habitually dishonest than to being habitually profane.

THE THIRD COMMANDMENT

TEXT: *Exodus 20:8-11*
"Remember the sabbath day, to keep it holy."

THE LOGIC OF THE FIRST THREE COMMANDMENTS is something like this: The basic obligation which rests upon man is that he shall acknowledge that he is a creature who is dependent upon and responsible to a Creator, God. There is among men a name by which that God is known. Men may know little or much about Him, but whatever they know about Him is signified and symbolized by that name. So there is a parallel between the reverence and respect which is shown to the Name and the reverence and respect which is felt for God. Now, just as there is a Name among all the names which we have given to people and to things which can be called the Lord's name, so there is a day which is called the Lord's day.

Although He is beyond all language—inscrutable and ineffable—yet there is a human word which is His name, which designates and represents Him in the world. Just so, although He is before and beyond history, the "eternal God," yet there is a day, a segment of history which can be measured by a clock and located on a calendar, which is His day. And just as what one does with God's name is an indication of one's own integrity and of his sincerity in acknowledging that he is a creature of God, so what one does with His day is a measure of one's obedience to this Lord throughout all days, all time, all history.

You might say that the holy Name, let down into the arena of the multitudinous voices by which we communicate with one another, is a sort of claim upon all language, upon all the arts and sciences, upon the spoken and the written word. Every word should be hallowed by that word which is the holy Name. And the holy Day, set into the cycle of each recurring week, is a sort of claim upon all days on the part of the holy God.

You may have observed that I have not up to this point made any reference to the Sabbath, but have spoken instead of the Lord's day. While not many of us are likely to be greatly troubled by the acknowledged fact that worship has been shifted from the last day of the week (Saturday) to the first day of the week (Sunday), and since most of us are willing to overlook that discrepancy, I think we ought to take a second look at it.

In the earliest references to the Sabbath, such as this one in Exodus, the motivation for the observance of the Sabbath is a sort of celebration of the completed work of creation. It is because the Lord had created the world in six days that the seventh day was to be a day of rest. But as one reads on in the Old Testament he discovers that the emphasis shifts to the deliverance out of Egypt and the founding of the Hebrew nation. Thus in Deuteronomy the people are admonished, "You shall remember that you were a servant in the land of Egypt, and the Lord your God brought you out thence with a mighty hand and an outstretched arm; therefore the Lord your God commanded you to keep the Sabbath." The prophet Ezekiel represents God as saying about it, "Moreover I gave them my sabbaths, as a sign between me and them, that they might know that I the Lord sanctify them." For the Israelites, the most important evidence, the irrefutable proof that God was at work in history, in this world of space and time, was that He had delivered them out of Egypt and fashioned them into a nation. Of this their weekly Sabbath was to remind them.

And then there came that day, as it began to dawn on the first day of the week, when Jesus of Nazareth arose from the dead, and was "designated Son of God in power . . . by his resurrection from the dead"—that was the way they put it. Here was an act of God, of divine deliverance, which dwarfed all others. Here was the most striking evidence of God's dominion over all the forces of nature and history and over all the enemies which were or could be arrayed against man. This central conviction that Christ was the victor and was with them still, despite the suffering and the dying, despite the perfidy and treachery and brutality of men—that He was still with them here and now in an eternal fellowship—this was the beginning of a new community of the believing and the faithful. This was a new day and they were a new people living under a new covenant. The day of His triumph became the holy Day which should stand as the constant reminder that all days and years are His. All time is a part of His dominion.

Remember the Sabbath Day to keep it holy. Remember that God is the Creator of your world and you. Remember that all the time you have, indeed all the time there is, is His. Remember the mighty acts of God in history, like the deliverance of His people out of Egypt and the founding of a nation. Perhaps it is not amiss either to remember the founding of our own nation as the product of such a mighty deed. But most of all, remember how the sinless and holy One of God "abolished death and brought life and immortality to light through the gospel." Take enough time away from the routines and responsibilities of your every day to focus your mind and heart on God, so that He can bring home to you that all your days belong to Him. It is a fatal error, in the end, to

25

think of your time as though it were your own. I think this is what Luther meant when he said, "We should so fear and love God, as not to despise His Word or the preaching of the gospel, but deem it holy, and willingly hear and learn it."

THE SECOND TABLE OF THE LAW

TEXT: *Deuteronomy 5:16-21*

THE FIRST AND FUNDAMENTAL COMMANDMENT is that we should love God; the simple and fundamental sin of man is that he loves himself instead. He asserts his own interests by a seemingly irresistible inner necessity. It is apparently natural for man to want to do as he pleases, even when his own will is set against the will of God.

A man who is responsive to no obligation beyond his own will, that is to say, a man who acts as though he were God and his world revolved around him, is a disruptive force in society. He is not only egocentric but *ec*centric—off center. He will jar the moorings of society; he will tear away at the fabric of a community's life together, and leave it in shreds. The kind of anarchy which results when every man does just as he pleases is fatal to the existence of any real community. This is the reason that the "first table of the Law," the first three Commandments, is concerned with putting God at the center of the universe and of each person's life.

Now, over against the disruptive force of egocentricity, God has set certain cohesive forces and factors which tend to hold the world together. There are bonds that resist the tendency to pull apart. They constitute a kind of counterbalance to the self-centeredness of man. They are not the product of man's decision or achievement, and they cannot be repealed or dissolved

27

by man. They may perhaps be weakened, but they will not utterly disintegrate and disappear. There are forces which, in spite of man's selfishness, drive men toward one another as well as forces which set them against one another. For instance, there is the fact that life is organized into families. You cannot rid the world of parents and children. You cannot fashion a world that will get along without parents and children. It is a law of creation, a necessity of existence, that there shall be a biological relation between one generation and the next.

There is some sense of the dignity and sanctity of life among all men. The desire to live involves some recognition of the right of others to live. In all societies this becomes a restraint, in some measure, on the taking of life. We appeal to it when we talk about humanitarianism and brotherhood. There is something in man which responds to that sort of appeal. We sometimes call it "the blood bond." And then there is the sex bond, that dynamic and dangerous force of which our generation has become almost neurotically aware, that strange and wonderful attraction by which two lives are led to yield up their separate existences to one another, and to accept as their own the needs and hopes of another.

And there is a force holding men together in the very fact of property, the fact of ownership. Sometimes ownership is thought of in terms of clan or tribe, as in much of the Old Testament and in many of the more primitive countries today, and sometimes in private or personal terms. In either case a social bond is involved in the existence of property. Respect for property rights, the world of trade and commerce, contracts and credits—everything that is derived from the existence of property—constitutes a cohesive force holding men together in some sort of community. This, of course, is not to deny that it is also an area in which the forces pulling men apart are also conspicuously present.

Language, too, is a bond that holds the world together. The

very fact that we can communicate with one another through the use of words makes possible a kind of community among humans which cannot exist among other forms of life. Even where differences in language divide, translation is possible, so that communication can still exist.

Now what does all of this have to do with the Ten Commandments? Just this: over each of these bonds by which the world is held together is set a Commandment. The God who created the world with these bonds built into it has defined our obligation toward Him and toward one another in such a manner as to safeguard and protect them. The Fourth Commandment stands guard, as it were, over the "family bond," "Honor thy father and thy mother"; the Fifth Commandment stands guard over the "blood bond," "Thou shalt not kill"; the Sixth Commandment stands guard over the "sex bond," "Thou shalt not commit adultery"; the Seventh Commandment stands guard over the "property bond," "Thou shalt not steal"; and the Eighth Commandment stands guard over the "language bond," "Thou shalt not bear false witness against thy neighbor." The Ninth and Tenth Commandments are refinements of the obligation to protect these bonds, with implications for each of them. As we concern ourselves with each of the Commandments, their particular relevance will be noted.

Perhaps this analysis of the second table of the Law will provide some indication of the kind of authority which they have. We are not bound by these Commandments because they have been spoken by Moses or by anyone else, but because they are the Law according to which God created the world in which we live. I suppose we could spend our lives trying to repeal them, but I'm afraid it's too late for that. It has been too late for that ever since the world began.

THE FOURTH COMMANDMENT

TEXT: *Exodus 20:12*
"Honor your father and your mother, that your days may be long in the land which the Lord your God gives you."

NOW WE WANT TO LOOK MORE CLOSELY at each of these Commandments in the second table of the Law, which have been set as sentinels to warn us of the points at which the social body must be protected, if it is not to be destroyed, and to remind us of the imperative obligations which must be assumed, if we are to be responsible persons in God's world.

This Commandment, the Fourth—that is the one which you are almost through with now, is it not? Most of you have left home in order to attend college and are to some degree, at least, on your own. You have almost reached your "maturity." Some of you have. Next to being "of age," perhaps the most effective way to shed your parents is to go away to school. But the time that is allowed us to enjoy this "man without a family" status is usually quite brief. Most of us are spared any prolonged indulgence of the adult privilege of acting childishly. Some of you who have attained some measure of freedom from responsibility to parents have already become involved with the Fourth Commandment again in the role of fathers and mothers to your own children. Even if one should resolutely embrace the state of "singleness" and independence in order to avoid involvement with the Fourth Commandment, he would surely not succeed. Those of you who have encountered Luther's *Small Catechism* somewhere in your religious training will recall that he interprets this Commandment so as to apply to all "superiors." It includes all who have some official relation of authority and responsibility in the ordering of society.

Moreover, there is this somewhat disturbing and highly intriguing promise attached to this commandment, "that your days may be long in the land which the Lord your God gives you." The Apostle Paul, writing in Ephesians, did not fail to note that this is "the first commandment with a promise." It is very interesting also to observe how he revises the statement of the promise so that it has more general and timeless reference—". . . that it may be well with you and that you may live long on the earth."

There are all kinds of interesting questions that come to mind at this point. Is it true that there is a correlation between long life and the proper recognition of duties and responsibilities as a member of a family? Do happy homes make for longevity? Why should there be a promise attached to this particular Commandment? Is it that this one is more difficult to perform than others so that some added inducement is needed? Is it so important that, even if one were to obey it for the sake of the reward rather than because it is right, it had better be done?

The whole question of the importance of the family in God's design is involved here. This is too big a matter to handle in a brief meditation. May I just point out that the family is the matrix out of which come all those attitudes and viewpoints and habits of action upon which the effective operation of all other groups depends. The family is creative of moral insight and understanding in a way that the economy or the political community can never be. Years ago, James Breasted wrote a book which he called *The Dawn of Conscience.*[1] In it he pushed back through early Egyptian history, beyond the Exodus and behind the days of Joseph and his brethren, to find the first written evidences of specifically moral judgments. He concluded on the basis of pictures and inscriptions on the walls of ancient Egyptian cemeteries that the first expressions of a sense of oughtness, of moral obligation, grew out of what he called "the delightful filial relations" between fathers and sons. Whether he was right or wrong, I do not know, but there is a real sense in which the "dawn of conscience" for each of us comes out of such family relationships.

Parental responsibility and concern, on the one hand, and the dependence and affection of children, on the other, have a biological and physiological basis which does not exist for any other group or order to which we may belong by nature or by choice. There is a moral dynamic in the family which is indispensable to the good life. Family life by its very nature requires us to take thought for others. Here, too, is conserved the moral experience and discernment of earlier generations, constantly infused and made alive by parental love and filial affection.

But there is always the possibility that we can dam up this stream of blessing, that we can turn off this current of moral insight, that we can sever the cord by which our moral lifeblood is supplied. We can do so by rebelling against, dishonoring, and being disrespectful toward, our parents. Blessed is that family where children honor their parents—and where the parents deserve it!

---

[1] James Breasted, *The Dawn of Conscience* (New York: Scribners, 1933)

THE FIFTH COMMANDMENT

TEXT: *Matthew 5:21-23*
"You shall not kill."

ONE WOULD HAVE TO BE INSENSITIVE indeed to stand at the point of birth or at the point of death, and not be greatly moved by a sense of the sacred mystery of life.

When a new life has come into your home—a new personality with whom one must enter into all kinds of relationships, and with whom one must always reckon when one thinks of one's family—then you have had an experience which cannot be shared by telling about it. There is a mystery and sanctity about it which only the most crude and callous could possibly miss. It derives from the awareness that even though we may be privileged to be called the parents of this one who has come to exist as a separate personality, life itself is a gift from God.

In the same way we become conscious of the mystery of life when we stand at the point of death. All of us stand often enough at the side of a body from which life has departed to keep some sense of its mystery alive in us. If we understood life, perhaps we would understand death, but we do in fact understand neither of them. Although we may puzzle more about death than about life, and hurl our questions and even shout our defiance at whoever or whatever presides over death, while we take life for granted, the mystery of birth and of death are exactly equal. The question, "Why do we die?" is of the same sort and of the same difficulty as the question, "Why are we born?"

In one sense it is not too difficult to convince a man that life is sacred, at least his life. It is an almost universal judgment that a man is fully justified in taking any action which is necessary to defend his life. If you were to ask people which of the Ten Commandments is the most important, the one which it would be most disastrous to have repealed, I expect that most people would select the Fifth Commandment. The killer is so obviously destructive and unfit for membership in any community that some method of separating him from the community is universal.

However, Jesus lifted this Commandment out of any narrow interpretation which would limit its reference to the obvious killer, and interpreted it so as to include all those attitudes and emotions which, if carried out to their fulfillment, would be destructive of another life. Anger, insolence, contempt, and hatred issue in violent death, if unrestrained. Whenever, therefore, we yield to these emotions, we are endangering another life. In principle, they desire the extinction or non-existence of another person, and therefore have much the same effect on us as though they were implemented and carried through. This is not to say that self-restraint is unimportant. The world would indeed be worse off if every thought issued in a deed. But, perhaps, we take too much comfort in the fact that we did not actually do what we had a mind to do.

Just as there is injury to another which we may desire but fail to carry out, so there can be injury to another which we do not consciously will, but which we do actually cause. What shall one say, for instance, of the carelessness and irresponsibility which endangers and sometimes destroys another life? The careening car that didn't quite make the curve, perhaps because of excessive speed, perhaps because the driver had been indulging his personal freedom to use intoxicants which slowed down his reactions so that he was not equal to the demands of modern traffic! The Mosaic Law defines some conditions under which the owner of the ox who gored a man or woman to death would himself be liable to the death penalty. Is not the modern motor car at least as much the instrument of the driver as the ancient ox? If we disregard those precautions and safety measures which are designed for the protection of life, we have to reckon with this Commandment.

There is, I suppose, one big question which cannot be avoided at this point. What about war and the Fifth Commandment? How shall we reconcile the wholesale destruction of life which war entails with this prohibition against the taking of life? I don't know that we can reconcile it. Perhaps we will just have to say that war is an illustration of how hopelessly tangled life can become among sinful men and nations, so tangled that there isn't any alternative to violating the commandments of God. But, presumably, the justification of war lies in defending one's life against the invader, a right which belongs to nations as to individuals. If there is to be any reconciliation between war and this Commandment, it will have to be on the premise that we do not act in war as individuals passing moral judgments on other individuals. We act in obedience to the decision of those in authority and are the instruments by which they carry out a responsibility, in behalf of all the citizens, which has been entrusted to them by the same God who has given us the Commandments. And the person on the other side, over against us, is not an individual either, but is, like us, the instrument of another's will. Some such resolution of the problem is necessary if one is conscientiously to participate in war.

Of course, there is a positive side to this Commandment. We are obedient only if we are helping our neighbor in every kind of need.

THE SIXTH COMMANDMENT

TEXT: *Ephesians 5:3-14*
"You shall not commit adultery."

UNDER ANY CIRCUMSTANCES one can expect to get a reasonable degree of attention from any group if he talks about sex. It is not least true of a student body. In some form or other it appears on almost every program that seeks to enhance its drawing power. It may be labelled, somewhat innocuously, "courtship and marriage," or "choosing a mate." In more sophisticated circles it is likely to be "sex education," "love and marriage," or some more dramatic and realistic phrase.

This is the age in which we have no inhibitions about sex, either in print or in the spoken word. We use the word almost as a badge of our emancipation. We have learned the techniques of "sex appeal," and have no hesitation in using them. Our advertisers capitalize on it as a kind of common currency which all people understand and to which they will respond.

There is something strikingly adolescent and unsophisticated about our contemporary preoccupation with sex. We almost give the impression that we think we invented it; or at least that it has just been discovered. Actually, it is as old as the human race, you know, and it is doubtful whether we have even added any perversions of it since Paul wrote the Epistle to the Romans.

For all of our brash conceit about our immense superiority over the generations that have preceded us, it is amazing how much we don't know about sex that is really worth knowing. Certainly it is not my purpose to minimize the importance and value of knowing about the physiology and psychology of sex, with all its historical and contemporary ramifications. But what I do want to assert is that what we are here talking about is the most intimate and personal and dedicated relationship which is available to man. Over this intimate and personal and dedicated relationship is set a Commandment which comes from God the Creator. This relationship can become the best or the worst. On the one hand, it can be a relationship of such exquisite beauty and grandeur that the New Testament does not hesitate to speak of the relationship between Christ and His Church in terms of the relationship between husband and wife, bride and bridegroom. On the other hand, it can be the most utter and awful violation of the very soul of another person.

Lust is not a kind of love; it is its counterfeit. It is therefore the enemy of love. Lust seeks to have its way with another; love "does not insist on its own way." To use another for one's own ends is always adultery, in the truest sense of the word, regardless of the level or the way in which we use him. But in no other way does one person so completely violate another as when he takes the most intimate and personal and dedicated of all human relationships and perverts it for his own personal gratification. This is adultery indeed.

The intimate and personal and dedicated nature of the sex relationship means that it must belong exclusively to the marriage relationship. No one has any right to share in the sex relationship who has not made a life-long commitment in marriage. Sometimes one actually encounters young folks who profess, at least, to believe that the commandment against adultery has reference only to unfaithfulness among married persons and to have no prohibition in it for unmarried persons.

Such naiveté is difficult to understand even in a sophisticated generation.

I wish I knew how to convince you, everyone, that God knew what He was talking about when He uttered this Commandment. It is not His way to deprive us of any good, but He does seek to save us from ourselves. There is something very profound in Paul's recognition that "fornication" is a sin against one's own body. The person who violates another also violates himself.

Of course, you can take the most precious things and make them cheap, if you want to. You can take the royal velvet of a king's robe, and make carpet rags out of it, but who would? You can take a diamond-studded bracelet, and make a drawer pull for the kitchen sink, if you want to, but who would? You can take a million-dollar bond and buy a dollar watch with it; but who would do that, except a fool who doesn't know the value of things? And you can take this intimate and personal and dedicated relationship which holds out the promise of being one of God's richest gifts to you, and you can cash it in for a moment's sensual gratification, but who would be such a fool as that?

There are many people talking and writing about sex today and not all of them come to the same conclusions. But there is only One who created it—and He says, "You shall not commit adultery." If you think otherwise, remember that you will have to reckon with Him.

THE SEVENTH COMMANDMENT

TEXT: *Exodus 20:15; Ephesians 4:28*
"You shall not steal."

I RECALL A LUNCHEON CONVERSATION with a well-known citizen of this State a couple of years ago which centered around the Declaration of Human Rights which has been drawn up under the auspices of the United Nations. This friend expressed his great surprise and his grave concern over the fact that the "right to property" had not been included among the fundamental human rights. It seemed to him to call into some question the validity of the entire document, and to cast some doubt on the direction which the United Nations seemed to be going.

Is the right to property a fundamental human right? It would seem to me to be a matter of some significance how one answers that question. We have said that one of the bonds which hold society together is the property bond. Although there may be tensions within an economic order, for instance between capital and labor, consumer and producer, still the net effect of any economic order is to make us dependent upon one another. Especially in a highly developed economic system is it necessary for us to trust one another. Credit is an important consideration.

In an economic order we are kept working not only for our own pleasure or profit, but we are kept productively engaged, doing something that serves some need in the total community of which we are a part. This is true regardless of the kind of economic system under which we live. To say this is not to say that all economic systems are equally good or valid. There is a great difference in their effectiveness as well as in the opportunity which they provide for those who live within them. But it is to say that economic systems take their origin in an inescapable dependence of one upon the other with reference to our material needs which has its basis in the way God created the world.

Whether or not the statement "What is mine is mine" can claim the status of a fundamental human right, the Seventh Commandment does assert that something like that must be said with regard to the statement "What is thine is thine." Perhaps no commandment is needed to prompt us to protect our own right to property. A commandment is needed to protect our neighbor's right to property. The whole of man's nature prompts him to acquire, but there is a commandment which sets limits upon his acquisitions. There are some things that belong to another. We must not take them from him.

The recognition that one can violate another's personality by taking from him that which is his seems important in the Scriptures. Not even a king has a right to take a poor man's sheep or his vineyard and treat it as though it were his own. The prophets are eloquent in their denunciation of those who acquire what is their neighbor's under the pretext of law.

I have a feeling that if we approach this matter of property by way of our neighbor's right to property rather than by way of our own right we will be on more solid ground. Of course, it is a fair inference that if our neighbor's right to property is to be protected, our right to property deserves the same consideration. Perhaps to insist on our neighbor's right is the surest way of insuring our own. We are so prone to claim our own rights, and so slow to protect the rights of others. And the development of responsible personality requires that we shall be responsible for some things which we are permitted to treat as our own. The right to property is the right to a home, to shelter, to food, and to clothing. It is the right of a person to apply his toil to his land, or whatever its equivalent may be, in order that he may provide for himself and his family. This right we must protect for our neighbor. God has set this Commandment before us to warn against trespassing upon that right.

It must be apparent to all of us that obedience to this Commandment in our highly developed and complicated economic society is by no means easy or simple. It involves all the questions of economic justice for all members in the productive enterprise, the interests of workers, employers, and consumers. But we are not excused from obedience to the Commandment because it has become difficult.

If we start at the point where we can do most about it, and do what we can there, we will be doing something about it everywhere. As members of a college community, do we ever take from another that which is his? Most often, I suppose, our offenses are against the group rather than against individuals. We have developed a curious notion in our modern world that what belongs to the community—the state, the government, the public, the school—everyone can make his own. Is not disregard for public property, whoever the public may be, a violation of the Seventh Commandment?

We have spoken almost entirely of thefts of property, but whatever our neighbor has a right to we must not treat as though it were ours. We can rob him of his time or his reputation. If we think the rights of our present neighbors are unimportant, and need not be protected, it is not likely that we will feel differently about any other neighbors, if they should have something that we want.

41

THE EIGHTH COMMANDMENT

TEXT: *Exodus 20:16; 23:1-3*
"You shall not bear false witness against your neighbor."

I WOULD NOT BE SURPRISED if there were those among you who are getting a bit impatient about these little homilies on the Ten Commandments. If you do find the Ten Commandments somewhat tedious and a bother, there is nothing very original about that. There is a great crowd—a "mighty host" you might say—who would gladly not hear of them again.

So this may be a good time to remind ourselves once more that a good deal of the significance of these particular Commandments is that they apply exactly as much even when we don't like them. They do not depend on our endorsement. They do not constitute some central core of man's wishes and hopes and longings which he is very reluctant to give up, and which he holds on to with some inexplicable tenacity. They are rather like the hard facts of life which one might very much want to get rid of, but which do not yield to our wishful thinking. They are like the rock strata that do not erode with the soil around them, and hence give the mountain its shape. There is something objective and enduring about them. One willful generation after another may wish to break loose, and fashion a world according to its own desires, but every new generation must still reckon with these Commandments as with a kind of ultimate authority.

It is fairly easy to see this truth with regard to killing or stealing or adultery. When one tampers with any one of these, he is quite obviously interfering with something essential to human society. It is not so easy to see it with regard to the Eighth Commandment, "You shall not bear false witness against your neighbor." How is a commandment like that inherent in the structure of things?

You remember we spoke of the bonds which hold society together: the family bond, the blood bond, the sex bond, the property bond, and the language bond. And then we said that over each of these bonds was set a commandment, to guard against the intruder and the invader. He who violates these bonds endangers the structure of the society in which he lives, and which is in some sense the work of the Creator. We suggested that the commandment which stands guard at the point of the language bond is this Eighth Commandment. Perhaps that seemed somewhat farfetched.

On a recent Sunday there was a wonderful television broadcast on deafness. It succeeded admirably in bringing the viewer into the world in which there are no words, and in depicting the loneliness and isolation of people who have no way of communicating with one another through the use of words. People who have lost their hearing, but who still have the power of speech, will tell you how they are shut off from any real community because, they are shut off from conversation. Often they grow suspicious of those who speak what they cannot hear, because they can never be quite sure that the laughter in which they cannot join is not directed against them. But to lose one's hearing cannot compare with never having heard. To have no knowledge of what sound is or of what words are or how to form them, this is surely to live in a world that withholds most of its secrets and much of its joys from us.

Words are precious things. You can penetrate to a man's

soul with words. You can put your knowledge into words, and share it with another. You can put truth into words, and give it wings. You can put your affection and esteem and devotion into words, and deliver them into the innermost citadel of the heart and mind of a loved one. But you can also put anger and bitterness and malice and envy and hatred into words, and they will pierce as deeply into the heart and mind as words of love and devotion. You can put the vilest, foulest lie into words, and it will travel even faster than the truth.

When our words become bearers of our bitterness, animosity, envy, pettiness, and hatred, we do all that we can to shatter and destroy one of the bonds that hold society together. We do such violence to the personality of another that we must reckon with God who created both him and us.

This Commandment should be thought of in relation to another commandment, the Second. God has a name, and you must not defile it by using it for purposes that are in conflict with His will and character. Your neighbor has a name. It is his very own. You must not defile it or defame it by slander, gossip, innuendo, or falsehood. God has set a guard around your neighbor's name as around His own.

We are prone to think lightly of words as compared to deeds, but words are deeds. They are the most revealing deeds in which we can be involved. "Out of the abundance of the heart his mouth speaks." There is a terribly earnest word of Jesus about it. He says, "I tell you, on the day of judgment, men will render account for every careless word they utter; for by your words you will be justified, and by your words you will be condemned." Which it will be depends on the kind of witness we have borne to God and to our neighbor.

THE NINTH AND TENTH
COMMANDMENTS

TEXT: *Exodus 20:17; Colossians 3:5; Ephesians 5:5*
"You shall not covet your neighbor's house."
"You shall not covet your neighbor's wife, or his manservant, or his maidservant, or his cattle, or anything that is your neighbor's."

THERE IS SOME JUSTIFICATION for treating the Ninth and Tenth Commandments together. Both of them enjoin us against "coveting." As you may know, there are two ways of dividing these Commandments into ten. One of them makes two out of what we have called the First Commandment, and combines what we have called the Ninth and Tenth into one. This is the reason that any reference to one of the Commandments in print is likely to elicit letters to the editor calling attention to the error in numbering, with some uncharitable reference to the deplorable ignorance which cannot even properly identify the Ten Commandments.

The question before us is, "What is wrong with coveting?" We may need to ask the prior question, "What is coveting?" If you have now settled back in the comfortable assumption that this chapel talk isn't going to concern you, may I hasten to urge that you are quite wrong about that. If I still have your ear, may I say, with shocking indelicacy, that you can go to hell for not knowing what covetousness is. You have

Paul's word for it that "no immoral or impure man, or one who is covetous (that is, an idolater), has any inheritance in the kingdom of Christ and of God." At this point, as at all others, ignorance of the Law which we should know and understand is no excuse.

There is always the danger that we generalize the meaning of the Commandments, and extend their implications so far that they lose their cutting edge. For instance, we may agree that we are all selfish and that this is contrary to God's Law: therefore we are all sinners. The commandment against covetousness is just another way of saying that selfishness is wrong. Of course, it is true that the essential sin of man is his selfishness. It is the desire to assert one's own will against the will of God. All particular sins are expressions of this basic rebellion. But there are varied expressions of the selfish spirit, and covetousness is one such expression which the Scriptures consider to be particularly dangerous and destructive.

It has been said about men that they are all "hunger points in the universe." We are bundles of drives, desires, urges, and instincts. These are like great generators in human lives, urging men forward and upward and outward. Perhaps without them no great thing would ever have been done. There have been men who thought they understood the will of God who have wanted to turn off these generators of human action, and reduce man to a completely passive creature without ambitions or desires. Sometimes they have even encouraged men to have contempt for the good earth and all that it contains, even contempt for their own bodies. But the mainstream of the Hebrew-Christian tradition has been "world-affirming" rather than "world-denying." This physical world may indeed be the place where the devil is encountered, but it is also the place where God is to be served. This world offers man an opportunity for true godliness, for it offers him the chance to serve his neighbor. It is not wrong that men shall have hopes and dreams and ambitions and desires. It is almost a condition of life itself that they shall have them.

But these desires and ambitions and longings can become wrong in two ways. (1) They become wrong when they are directed toward that which is another's. It's dangerous to let that happen. In and of itself there is nothing wrong with wanting to possess something—a precious stone, a house, a car, a plot of land. But when what one wants to possess is another's, the relationship shifts from a relationship between a person and a thing to a relationship between a person and another person. The desire for the thing becomes a desire directed against the person who owns it. It should not be necessary to say that there is here nothing to enjoin us against commerce or trade. When we mutually agree with our neighbor to exchange the money that is ours for the house that is his, we have in no sense violated this Commandment merely because we wanted what was his enough to make the exchange. But we are forbidden to seek to get something for nothing, by craftiness or deceit. The recognition that some things belong to others, and that their rights are to be protected, is essential to any true community. It is also essential to disciplined and contented living.

(2) The second way in which desire and ambition become wrong is that we fasten upon the good things of life as though they were ends in themselves. You remember, the Apostle Paul keeps referring to covetousness as "idolatry." It was Emerson who said, "Things are in the saddle and ride mankind." Ours is an age in which things may be more important in the minds of men than at any other time in Christian history. Our culture is an economic culture more than we recognize or will admit. The hazards of wealth are hazards which most of us would be glad to confront. But we can pray real and honest prayers for deliverance from the hazards of poverty.

I have a feeling that if we were wiser than we are, we would busy ourselves much with understanding this Commandment about coveting. It seems so harmless to us that it could very well be the rock on which we are most likely to stumble and fall. We pride ourselves that America has grown strong on free enterprise, unlimited opportunity, and wholesome ambition. There is much truth in it, and it is not wrong to be grateful that we have enjoyed an economic system that has been well suited to the development of American resources and to the achievement of high standards of material well-being. But I am increasingly convinced that private giving has been as important in this development as private getting. Free institutions, voluntarily supported, have been an important element in "the American way." By keeping sensitive people aware of the needs of others, and the necessity of using their physical means in this service, they have helped to save us from the worst excesses of a commercial civilization.

If we are wise, we will flee covetousness as a plague, for it is the disease which is most indigenous to an economic culture. How to save ourselves and our society from it may well be the most important task before us. The distance between the highest standard of living in the world and that covetousness which is idolatry may be shorter than we think.

PART TWO

The
Apostles' Creed

I BELIEVE . . .

TEXT: *Hebrews 11:1-3*

IN WHATEVER CHURCH YOU MAY HAVE WORSHIPED, and in whatever church you will worship in the future, you will at some time join in saying the Apostles' Creed. It is called one of the "ecumenical creeds," which means that it is confessed by Christians everywhere. Not everyone may take it seriously, but at least nominally, everyone who wants to be known as a Christian affirms this Creed. It is called the Apostles' Creed not because it was written by the original apostles, but because it embodies the faith of the original Christian community.

The word "creed" comes from the Latin *credo* which means, "I believe." What follows is a confession of faith—that faith which was proclaimed by those who went out to bear the gospel to the nations.

It is important to keep in mind that this is the creed of apostles. It might be interesting to speculate how it would have been written, if it had been compiled by the lawyers or by philosophers. The lawyers might have written it something like this:

Whereas the opinion that there is a God is prevalent in a large portion of the human populace; and

Whereas this opinion has been prominently held for many centuries; and

Whereas there is no overwhelming evidence adduced to the

contrary whereby a departure from well-established precedent would be justified;

Therefore, be it affirmed that there is a God.

The philosophers might have put it something like this:

The idea of God is an idea than which no greater idea can be conceived;

That which exists in reality is greater than that which exists as an idea;

Therefore, God must exist in reality, since otherwise the most perfect idea would have no counterpart in reality, and hence could not be the most perfect idea.

Indeed, certain philosophers have expressed it in those words.

But the apostle says quite simply, "I believe in God." With him it is not a conclusion that comes at the end of a series of arguments. It is a starting point. His faith in God is not a consequence of what he believes about other things, but rather what he believes about other things is a consequence of what he believes about God.

I want to say two things about faith before we begin to talk about Him in whom we believe. The first thing is that faith is not a lower kind of knowledge. Faith is not an uncertain attitude, a kind of surmise that something may be true. It is not a way of saying, "I think perhaps this may be true." The writer to the Hebrews says, "Faith is the assurance of things hoped for, the conviction of things not seen." It is assurance and it is conviction. The testimony of the senses could not add anything to the certainty of faith. When the Christian says, "I believe in God," he is making the most confident affirmation of which he is capable.

The other thing I want to say is that when we speak of knowledge and faith as in some sense opposites, we are talking about the way we know, rather than the certainty of our knowledge. When we want to express the highest degree of confidence with reference to some thing, we say, "I know this is true." But when we want to express the highest degree of confidence with reference to a person, we say, "I believe in him." That is why, when we want to express our confidence in God, we say, "I believe . . ."

When it seems to men that they can get along without faith, it is not because they have learned so much that faith has become a sort of surplus article. It is rather because they have come to look at the world around them as though it consisted only of things, not of persons. God is reduced to a force or energy or law or problem. How often in a college community God is regarded as a problem! Perhaps the endless round of student discussions dealing with the problem of God is not wasted; the student mind is not unprofitably employed when it is wrestling with the idea of God.

But we do not know God as a result of all this discussion. We know Him only when we have encountered Him, when we have met Him as a Person who confronts us and calls upon us to respond to Him as we respond to persons. When we know Him thus, and want to express our confident trust in Him, it will not be enough to talk about the things we know about Him. We will have to say with the Christian Church through the centuries, "I believe in God."

It is the purpose and task of this institution of Christian higher education not only to clarify and validate your ideas about God, but also, and most important, to provide the environment and the conditions in which you may encounter Him.

. . . IN GOD, THE FATHER ALMIGHTY

TEXT: *Psalm 91*

I TRIED IN THE PREVIOUS MEDITATION to give some concrete content to the words with which the Creed begins—"I believe"—by indicating that faith does not mean uncertainty or some lower form of knowledge. Rather it expresses assurance and conviction with regard to a person as ordinary knowledge involves assurance and conviction with regard to a fact.

That is why our certainty about God is most appropriately expressed in the confession, "I believe in God." God is a Person. Today we must go on to say that He is not just any person, but a Person who is in some unique fashion entitled to be designated as the Father of all men and who, unlike the fathers that we know, exercises complete authority and unlimited dominion over His family.

Some years ago a very clever philosopher wanted to remake the conception of God by substituting another name for "God." He felt that people had so many wrong notions about the nature of the divine Being that it was hopeless to try to purify the meaning of the word "God." He suggested that we discard the word altogether, and substitute for it the Latin verb "to be," which is *"sum."* I presume that he would have given it a capital letter, *"Sum."* Now, I think that only a very young man, whose cleverness outweighed his wisdom, could ever seri-

54

ously have proposed such a venture or expected to be successful in it. The word *"Sum"* might indeed be an acceptable substitute for "God," providing that it meant to us what "God" means to us. You may remember that the Hebrew word for God has roots in the Hebrew verb "I am." But one must have an unusual amount of credulity, and more ignorance of history than should fall to the lot of any one man, to assume that he can make the name of God, or the divine Being, mean anything that he wants it to mean. No man invented the idea of God, and no man can invent another idea called *"Sum,"* and tell us what it ought to mean. It is not thus that humanity has come to its knowledge of God.

Men have come to their knowledge of God through their long and lonely encounter with Him. He has met them even when they were not seeking Him, and subdued them until they came to trust and obey Him. The record of man's encounter with God reaches back to the beginning of life. The road on which they have met Him is as wide as the wanderings of the human race, and as deep as the wounded soul. Men have sensed His presence in the shattering storm and the raging sea, as they came to understand that they were pitted against a power that was not their own and one stronger than they. They have seen glimpses of Him in the majestic beauty of the stars and in the splendor of the sunset and the sunrise. They have sensed His presence in the fall of empires and in the preservation of a remnant from the oppressor. Most of all, they have wrestled with Him in their own souls. They have heard His voice speaking in accents of authority, the still small voice within, and the mighty thunders in nature and in history. They have heard Him call them to accept responsibility for their neighbor, the claim of justice—and more than justice, mercy. Those who listened came to understand that there was a dominion and a power which they did not create and which they could not destroy. Not infrequently, He has spoken and men have heard His voice most clearly in the silence of defeat, disaster, and death. And all through this long history of the human sojourn, there have been those who were obedient to as much of God as they knew, and who have learned more because of it. A Moses, a David, a Hosea, an Isaiah, and all the rest whose insight and understanding have helped us all in our encounter with the only God there is!

In no other area of our knowledge are we indebted to so long a past as in our knowledge of God. From the beginning God has been revealing himself to men, asserting His authority and exercising His dominion over them. Wherever men have had any knowledge of God, it has been because they were obedient to that authority and dominion. Through the First Article of the Creed we affirm the faith of believers throughout all ages who have responded to as much as they knew about "God, the Father Almighty."

Of course, as Christians we affirm more than those who have not seen "the light of the glory of God in the face of Jesus Christ." We worship a God who is "the Father of our Lord Jesus Christ." But this is the confession which is contained in the Second Article. Here, I think, we will not go far wrong, if we let the emphasis rest upon God as the Father of all men, who has not left himself without a witness anywhere in the human family.

One thing more: The first and great commandment, as Jesus defined it, is that we shall love the Lord our God with all our heart and strength and mind and soul. The First Article of the Creed is the answer of faith to that commandment. Faith is the appropriate response of love toward God. To surrender willingly and confidently to His authority and dominion is to believe in Him. We do not prove our love for Him by offering Him something else, but by yielding ourselves to His will.

THE FATHER ALMIGHTY, MAKER OF
HEAVEN AND EARTH

TEXT: *Genesis 1:1; Isaiah 42:5-8*

GOD THE FATHER IS NOT ONE FATHER AMONG MANY; He is the Father of all men. His power is not one power among other powers; He is the Almighty One. Both of these aspects of God are asserted when we say that He is the "Maker of heaven and earth."

If by the term "Almighty" one must understand that all that happens in the world is the simple product of His will, in a fatalistic manner, then it would appear that the Christian Church has been ill-advised in describing God in such terms. I am sure that countless student hours have been spent in weighing the evidence for and against God's omnipotence on the assumption that it must mean something like that.

It is always dangerous to assume that an earlier generation, and particularly many generations, have been less bright than we are. The Christian Church has been much aware that there is another will at work in the world. Indeed, earlier generations have been much more aware of the devil than our own generation is. There is opposition to God in the world, and the opposition is not a kind of stage play—it is real. But God reveals that He is the Almighty precisely in relation to this opposition. He is the Lord of hosts who triumphs over the hosts of the evil one. He triumphs even when He seems to lose—as on the cross—because He can also win with the weapons of love. In the end, it will be God and not His enemy that will prevail.

And what the Christian faith asserts about the final outcome is rooted, at least in part, on what it believes about the beginning. The Almighty God is the "Maker of heaven and earth." The doctrine of creation is a statement of faith. It cannot be proved either by logic or by historical evidence. There are very respectable arguments that may be used in support of it, to be sure. For instance, there is the argument that since every known effect has a cause, there must be a First Cause which is adequate to account for all the effects, and that only God is such an adequate First Cause. There is the argument that since the world seems to have some design, there must have been a Designer. The existence of a watch argues for the existence of a watchmaker. But the Christian faith in the Creator does not rest upon these arguments. When we say that we believe in "God, the Father Almighty, Maker of heaven and earth," we are not only saying that we believe this is the kind of world which needs a "Maker" but we are also saying that we know the kind of God who makes heaven and earth.

If that seems like a meaningless distinction, let me assure you that it is not. Most of the religions of the world have been able to believe in a god or gods without believing that the world was his or their creation. In general, they have followed one of two patterns. Either they have believed that the inner nature and essence of the world was a kind of extension of the divine being, or they have believed that it was something wholly foreign to the divine being—the work of a hostile power and in its nature, evil. There was an early Christian heresy which tried to set the Creator God against the God who was the Father of our Lord Jesus Christ. Those of you who are students of church history will recall that the Christian Church has had to do battle against both of these views in order to safeguard its doctrine of creation, and its faith in the Creator.

Against the first of these, the doctrine of creation asserts that this world is not divine or eternal. Against the second, it asserts that this world is the handiwork of God himself, and is in its nature good, however perverted it may have become through the abuse of men.

It is not possible here to explore all the implications of the doctrine of creation for the Christian student. But I would make two further observations. The first is that it is not enough to think of God's creative activity as though it belonged to the past alone. It is not true merely that God was the Creator, who in the beginning created a world and then retired from the scene; He is the Creator still. This day is as much the product of His creative work as the first day. Yesterday is not the parent of today, nor does today have the creative power to give birth to tomorrow. If God were not now creating, the world would cease to be.

The second observation is this: If God is the Creator, as well as the Redeemer, we cannot ever rid ourselves of our dependence upon Him. There may be a sense in which we can choose whether or not we are to be among His redeemed, but we cannot choose whether or not we are to be one of His creatures. He has created us, and this makes us forever dependent upon Him for our very being. Whether we like it or not, we are part of His dominion, and we must answer before Him who is our Creator, as He is the "Maker of heaven and earth."

I BELIEVE IN JESUS CHRIST

TEXT: *Matthew 16:13-17*

THE SECOND ARTICLE OF THE CREED began with that somewhat rash and daring declaration of Peter at Caesarea Philippi,
"You are the Christ, the Son of the living God." Perhaps he
did not understand all that his words meant, but it is likely
that he had a clearer impression of what was implied in this
announcement than do most of those who today repeat the
substance of his confession in the words of the Apostles'
Creed.

There is real drama in this brief narrative. We may miss
the simplicity and splendor of it because we do not quite believe the "humanness" of it. A fisherman and a carpenter had
become close friends. The circumstances under which they had
come to know one another had involved fishing boats and fishing nets, evenings along the shore of Galilee and in the city of
Capernaum, a few visits in the fisherman's home, and some
introductions to his relatives and friends—associations that were
perfectly normal and familiar to many people in similar circumstances. Perhaps the impression which the carpenter had
made on the fisherman was somewhat unusual. Peter had come
to believe in him to the extent that he left his fishing boats
and business to travel in the company of this carpenter-teacher.
He found a kind of satisfaction in this fellowship which made

60

him loath to leave the company of the carpenter and his friends. It was a manly, masculine sort of friendship with strong attachment on both sides, despite the fact that they were quite different from one another. Indeed, one would have to say that Peter was being both attracted and repelled by the carpenter. He was being led along a road which was not native to him and he did not always approve of it. If anyone had asked him to account for his behavior, he would most likely have had to admit, in some form or other, that he "believed" in Jesus.

So far, I think, the experience is not wholly unique. Other teachers have had disciples. Perhaps you have some teacher whom you trust implicitly; you take everything he says at face value; you find yourself governed by what he says and does. It may be someone who isn't on any faculty, but who has accredited himself to you as one in whom you could not but believe. There is something sacred and awful about a relationship like that. It is an incalculably precious thing to a teacher to realize that he can inspire confidence in his person, so that the truth which he declares finds a readier access into another mind. But it is awful, too, for such confidence extends to the error and ignorance of the teacher as well. The wise student will not trust his teacher absolutely—he will allow for a margin of error.

But something happened to Peter's faith in Jesus which never happens to our faith in a friend. One day Peter the fisherman became convinced that Jesus the carpenter was God. This human fellowship between two men had become a divine-human fellowship that included God. Can you imagine what it would be like? Think of your own best friend! Suppose that one day you should really become convinced that this friend is God! Try to imagine that! The fellowship wouldn't be the same any more; it would not be a fellowship between equals. This friend—one with the Sovereign God, the Creator and the Lord, who holds the destiny of all men in His hand, the Lord and Giver of Life—and still your friend! But now it would be dependent on His will to continue the friendship; you could make no claim upon it.

I am sure that I can speak for all when I say that, no matter how highly we prize our dearest friends, even the suggestion that one of them might turn out to be God is disturbing and somewhat shocking. Our friends are too imperfect even to pretend to play the role of God. But this only serves to emphasize the startling character of Peter's confession, which now seems commonplace as we "recite" the Second Article of the Apostles' Creed.

The insight which came to Peter, and which he expressed so recklessly, is the insight which has come to all Christians. They have learned about Jesus of Nazareth, and it has finally come to them with an overwhelming and unanswerable conviction that He is the Christ, the Son of the living God. That is, they have become convinced that God is like Jesus Christ, so like Him that there can be no sharp line drawn between them. For Peter, God had come to wear the face of Jesus Christ. He would never be able to think of God without thinking of Jesus. As Paul put it later, he had come to see "the light of the knowledge of the glory of God in the face of Christ." When you look into the face of Jesus, you are looking into the face of God. The searching, compassionate, and forgiving eyes of Jesus are the eyes of God himself. When God speaks to the world, He speaks with the voice of Jesus. God stands for the things Jesus stood for. God is trying to get done the things that Jesus was trying to get done.

Now if men want to know what God is like, you don't need to come up with an argument or a list of "the attributes of God." You can point men to Jesus of Nazareth who is the Christ. God has been here. We know what He did, and we know what He said. His footprints are on "the sands of time."

. . . HIS ONLY SON . . .

TEXT: *Matthew 13:54-58; 14:33*

WHEN WE WANT TO IDENTIFY OURSELVES, we will normally do so by declaring our identity with a family. There will be a few close friends for whom it will be sufficient to say into the telephone, "This is John." For most callers it will be necessary to add a family name—Peterson, Brown, or Schmitt. And because there are so many of them, you may have to specify which one by identifying the town in which you live or the business with which you are associated. We are so much a part of the family to which we belong that we carry around with us as a part of our own identification the name of the family, as well as our own name.

It was true of Jesus, too. His neighbors knew Him as "the carpenter's son." They knew His mother, Mary, and His brothers, James, and Joseph, and Simon, and Judas. We wish we knew more about that home. The New Testament tells us a little; our knowledge of Biblical times enables us to conjecture a good deal more. The few snatches of the story preserved in the New Testament reveal the strange circumstances of His birth, with their hint of glory and their promise of pain that would pierce like a sword through a mother's heart. There is the visit to the temple in Jerusalem at the age of twelve, a few references to His mother and His brothers—that is about all. But we do know that the relationships within that home were such that the dying Son did not forget to arrange for His

63

mother's care, and the words "father" and "brother" which Jesus, too, had learned first in the relationships of a human family, were to Him words that could describe God's relationship to Him and to all men, and His own relationship to every man. He found no difficulty, apparently, in transcribing the language of the Nazareth household into the language of "the household of faith."

But the family of Jesus does not at all account for Him. You cannot say about Him, as you can about many people, that having met His family you can understand Him better. People had trouble really getting to know Jesus because they were unable to think of Him apart from that family that they knew so well. "Is not this the carpenter's son? . . . Where then did this man get all this?" they said. Jesus himself must have realized early that He would have to put His life in a larger context than that of the family in Nazareth. Perhaps He was already aware of it when His parents found Him in the Temple at the age of twelve and He answered their anxious questions with the words, "How is it that you sought me? Did you not know that I must be in my Father's house?" Surely He knew it when His mother and brothers came to take Him home in response to the twisted rumors that had come to them. It was a strange way to greet that family from Nazareth—"Who are my mother and my brothers? . . . Whoever does the will of God is my brother, and sister, and mother." He seemed to be consciously cutting himself off from that family with which His neighbors associated Him, and attempting to help people to see that He would have to be understood as a part of another family.

With increasing boldness and growing earnestness He kept asserting that there was another family, another kinship, that was of decisive importance if one were to understand who He was and what He was doing in the world. When Peter had glimpsed the face of God in the face of the carpenter, Jesus, he boldly declared, "You are the Christ, the Son of the living God." Jesus did not rebuke him for it, but confirmed his judgment as coming from "my Father who is in heaven." If we are to take the Scripture record at all seriously, we cannot avoid the conclusion that Jesus claimed a unique relationship to God, and that He described that relationship in terms of the relation of a Son to His Father.

But how are we to understand that claim, which the church affirms in the confession that Jesus Christ is God's "only Son, our Lord"? Perhaps we could put it into this kind of assertion: Jesus Christ belongs by nature to the family of God as completely as we belong by nature to the family of man. We do recognize our kinship with every man. Somewhere, at the center of our being, we are like all men. And Jesus recognized His place with all men as "the carpenter's son." But, whereas it is part of that humanity which we share with all men that we are *not* by nature of the family of God, but rather stand over against Him as creatures and sinners, Jesus recognized precisely the opposite. He knew himself to be on the side of God. He did not share in the rebellion of the human heart against its Maker. He said, "I always do what is pleasing to him." "My food is to do the will of him who sent me." You will search in vain through the Scriptures for any evidence of the consciousness of guilt in Jesus. "Which of you convicts me of sin?" He could ask, with no fear that the challenge would be taken up. With equal confidence He said, "Let him that is without sin among you be the first to throw a stone at her." If there were no other evidence of Jesus' divinity than this consciousness that He was at one with God in a way that we are not, we would have no recourse but to say that Jesus belongs over on the side of God in a way that we do not. He is divine, as we are human.

We, too, are permitted to enjoy the status of sons in the Father's kingdom, but ours is an adopted sonship. It is characteristic of our adopted sonship that the closer we come to God—the better we know Him—the more we realize that we are sinners who stand over against Him, and must be redeemed by His love. For Jesus, and for Jesus only, it was not so. The ancient creeds, such as the Nicene, speak of the Son as being "of one substance with the Father." Something like that needs always to be said, lest we make of Jesus something less than He is. But we must not yield to the temptation to define God as though we knew Him apart from Jesus Christ. Neither should we think of Him in too "substantial" terms. If God is Spirit, then it is the heart and will and mind of God that is His "substance." Luther was content to say, "We find the heart and will of the Father in Christ." If we find that, it is enough.

There is another implication of the word "only," when we confess our faith in Jesus as God's "only Son." We have said that He alone of all men was so identified with God that there was nothing that stood between them. Therefore He is the agent and the embodiment—the incarnation—of God's love. And there is a finality, a completeness, about that revelation which precludes the possibility of another "Son of God." For the Christian Church, Jesus Christ is God. He is what the church means by God. One might almost as well look for a fuller revelation of Abraham Lincoln than Abraham Lincoln was. Another man might look like Lincoln, but he could hardly look more like Lincoln than Lincoln did. Similarly, the Christian Church which believes in Jesus Christ, God's only Son, "who reflects the glory of God and bears the very stamp of his nature," cannot acknowledge the possibility of a fuller revelation of God than it now has. It is meaningless to speak of another Son, another Christ; one can only speak of a Christ who will come again.

. . . OUR LORD

TEXT: *1 Timothy 6:13-16*

THERE ARE REASONS FOR BELIEVING that the earliest Christian confession consisted of the simple affirmation, "Jesus Christ is Lord." For instance, Paul writing to the Romans seems to imply this when he says, "If you confess with your lips that *Rom 10:9* Jesus is Lord and believe in your heart that God raised him from the dead, you will be saved." In writing to the Corinthians he reminds them that "no one can say 'Jesus is Lord' except by the Holy Spirit." One can find other echoes, too, throughout the New Testament.

In that Creed which embodied the faith of the apostles, the church proclaimed and continues to proclaim its conviction that Jesus Christ is not only God's "only Son," but also "our Lord." When Luther wanted to put the faith which is affirmed in the Second Article of the Creed in the briefest possible compass and the simplest possible language, he said, "I believe that Jesus Christ . . . is my Lord."

Still, it is probably true for most Christians in our time—perhaps even for us—that this is one of the weakest and least definitive titles which we can use of Him who is the center of our faith and of our hope. When we speak of "the Lord Jesus" we are as likely as not to be thinking of the word "Lord" as little more than an adjective which connotes respect and perhaps a measure of affection. Indeed, if we were to use the simplest and most ordinary word for what we mean when we say "Lord Jesus" we would probably say "Dear Jesus." The affection which we thereby express may be commendable, but it is an almost pitiful dilution of what the title actually means.

We live in an era—perhaps near the end of an era—that has been characterized by a general revolt against authority and the assertion of the autonomy of man. "Lords" are relics of the past. We have made ourselves free from such "overlords" as made the title exceedingly meaningful to the first disciples and to Christians in many countries during most of the history of the church. Along with them have gone many of the disciplines of life as well. Perhaps we have been willing to retain the title for Jesus because we do not take His "Lordship" seriously.

If we did really take it seriously, this simple affirmation that "Jesus is Lord" would come to us with the impact of the crack of doom—and the crack of dawn. For what is really asserted is that Jesus Christ is Lord in a sense which has no earthly parallel. He is the "Lord of lords."

All the authorities and dominions which we know in this world can exercise only a limited lordship. For instance, they are limited in duration. They last for a while only. We are under parents, but we will grow up and no longer be under their authority. We are under teachers, but the time will come when we will be out of school and then we will be free. We may be under political tyranny now, as many Christians around the world are, but some day we shall be free. This conviction that the tyranny cannot last for long, and certainly not forever, has helped many a suffering community. If not before, we shall be free from the tyrants in death. Men have given their lives for a variety of causes in the calm confidence that they would be vindicated beyond the reach of the tyrant's heel.

But you never grow up out of the dominion of Christ. You can't get rid of His Lordship by growing old—not even by dying. Especially not by dying! For death is precisely the place where the controls of life move out of your hands— into His. We shall stand at the last with no life or power or choice, except that which He is willing to give us.

These earthly dominions are limited in scope, too. You can move outside of their jurisdiction. You can leave home, quit school, move out of the country. This freedom gives a kind of veto power which stands over against the power of the rulers. But you can't move outside of the dominion of Jesus Christ. There is no place that is outside of His jurisdiction. "Whither shall I flee from thy presence?" "That at the name of Jesus every knee should bow, in heaven and on earth and under the earth." At the end there is no refuge from Him; only refuge in Him.

These earthly dominions are limited, too, in how much of us they can command. They may tax our purses, they may govern our time, they may control our actions, but they cannot govern our wills. They may discipline our outer man, but they cannot command our spirits. We will think what we want to think, we will believe what we want to believe. These alien powers cannot command the inner citadel which is our true self. But if you have encountered Jesus at all, you know that He will have none of that. It is precisely there, at the center of our selves, that He would rule. His Word is sharp to discern the thoughts and intents of the heart. The weapons of the divine warfare which are in the hands of Christ and His disciples "have divine power to destroy strongholds" and to "take every thought captive to obey Christ."

From all earthly dominions there is an appeal. It is surely a mark of great progress in human history that we have recognized the fallibility of human judgment, and have sought to protect ourselves and our fellows from it by providing for a system of appeals all the way up to the United States Supreme Court. And he who serves the cause of truth and right may need to remember that there is a tribunal that is even beyond the highest human court. There are many who have been called upon to serve a higher justice than that which has found expression in the judicial system of their land. But there is no appeal above and beyond the Lordship of Jesus Christ. The Father has committed all judgment into His hands. To Him has been given *all* authority in heaven and on earth.

From such a Lord it is small wonder that men flee, or try to turn Him into an option which they may choose if they feel like it. When we try to turn Him into a Lord whom we may choose, we assert our freedom from Him, even as we profess to surrender to Him. But the Lordship of Christ means that He is not one of our choices. He is the Lord, whether we choose Him or not. From Him there is no escape. We can only choose whether we will be His obedient or His disobedient servants.

It is our good fortune that He who is this kind of Lord, "the blessed and only Sovereign, the King of kings and Lord of lords," is also incarnate Love! He has taken the sins and failures of all mankind upon himself, as though they were His own. How can we thank God sufficiently for this great gift—that He who is our Lord is our Redeemer, too?

WHO WAS CONCEIVED BY THE HOLY GHOST, BORN OF THE VIRGIN MARY

TEXT: *Matthew 1:18-25*

THERE ISN'T ANY SUCH THING AS AN ORDINARY BIRTH or an ordinary child—not to parents, at least. Anyone who has had the holy privilege of holding a child in his arms for the first time and saying, "This is my child," understands that there never was nor can be a child just like this one. Two streams of human life have flowed together to bring into existence a new person. No other streams of life could bring this person into being. And even a brother or sister, uniting the same streams of life, would still be another person, perhaps astonishingly unlike this one. The mystery of that uniqueness which belongs to each new life, and the glory of it, cannot be dispelled by any explanation which the textbooks offer.

But there is another and greater mystery that attaches to the uniqueness of the Babe of Bethlehem. Here is something more than the merger of separate human streams; here is the merger of the human and the divine. This is what the church asserts in its confession that Jesus Christ was "conceived by the Holy Ghost, born of the Virgin Mary." If one does not accept the claim that Jesus belongs over on the side of God—that He is God—the doctrine of the Virgin Birth will be neither relevant nor meaningful. Christians do not believe that Jesus is

71

God because they believe in the Virgin Birth. They believe in the Virgin Birth because they believe that Jesus is God. The Virgin Birth is not an argument or a proof for the divinity of Christ. It is rather intended as an acknowledgment of the mystery which lies about the birth of Christ, just as the confession of His resurrection acknowledges the mystery which lies about His departure from this life. It asserts that Christ is a miracle. You cannot account for Him by the streams of human ancestry which lie behind Him. Here is the merger of the human and the divine. While the mystery of new life can never be explained, this mystery cannot even be described. The only name that can be given to it is "miracle."

There are those who stumble at this miracle. I would remind you, however, that we are not spared from believing in a miracle by the simple expedient of rejecting the Virgin Birth. The real miracle, the inexplicable mystery, is how God could unite himself with man. The theologians and philosophers sometimes discuss the question of whether the "finite can contain the infinite." How can God be man? Here is the real obstacle for all who would explain Jesus Christ. It is no easier to explain or describe it if one assumes that He somehow became God during His life than it is to explain "conceived by the Holy Ghost, born of the Virgin Mary."

But it must be equally insisted that the doctrine of the Virgin Birth is not an explanation of how God could unite himself with man. It is not intended to dispel the mystery that attaches to Christ's birth. Sometimes this doctrine has been treated as though it were an explanation, and one could proceed to argue from it to make other assertions about the relation between the human and the divine in Christ. Rather, the doctrine of the Virgin Birth is an assertion that you cannot account for Jesus by the ordinary processes of human generation. You cannot find the adequate cause for the person, Jesus, in any human ancestry. Jesus is God. The meaning of His life is that God has invaded human life and history. You cannot account for His origin without reference to God's own action and initiative, any more than you can account for the way He lived and died and rose again.

There is, I suppose, a question that must be raised. Is it really true that Jesus had no earthly father? May not the church have merely used this doctrine to state its faith in the divine-human origin of Him whom it acknowledges to be both God and man? There are only two authentic witnesses with regard to the question, Joseph and Mary. There are good reasons for believing that the account in Luke's Gospel comes from Mary and that the account in Matthew's Gospel comes from Joseph. Both accounts agree on the answer. Mary found that she was to become a mother "before they had come together." One would seem to need very good witnesses to outweigh what appears to be the testimony of Mary and Joseph.

Personally, I would have to say that if Joseph and Mary had testified differently, or if they had been silent about the matter altogether, I should still believe as firmly that the Child of Bethlehem was the Son of God. He is the miracle, however He came into the world. Among miracles one is not more probable than another. All are impossible—except to God.

I believe that Jesus Christ was "conceived by the Holy Ghost, born of the Virgin Mary" because I believe that He is the Son of God.

SUFFERED UNDER PONTIUS PILATE

TEXT: *Luke 23:24, 25*

IF IT WERE NOT THAT WE HAVE REPEATED it so often that
our sensibilities have been somewhat dulled, we would be
startled and even shocked by that sudden transition in the Creed.
In one sentence we confront "God's only Son, our Lord" who
came into the world by a divine miracle, "conceived by the
Holy Ghost, born of the Virgin Mary." And then, without
warning or preparation, we pass over to what seems to deny
all of that—"suffered . . . crucified . . . dead . . . buried."

The Biblical record tells us much of what Jesus said and
did, and most of it reflects the glory that one might have expected from the lips of so great a King, so royal a Guest in
human history. There is the story of the angel visitors, the
worshiping shepherds, the wise men from the East—and this
we feel instinctively is as it should be. The wisdom that He
revealed in the Temple at the age of twelve, the parables of
consummate beauty which speak so simply and so eloquently
to all time, the miracles of power in which He stilled the
waves and demonstrated His dominion over the hazardous
forces of nature and the malignant forces of disease and even
death—these are such as one might expect from so royal a
Visitor to these human shores.

And yet, there is nothing about all of this in the Creed. One
might have expected it to be there. Surely its absence does

not imply that the Christians of the early centuries did not believe what the Bible contains about Jesus' life. But it does seem to imply that the definitive and decisive thing about the Christian's faith is not how he reacts to Jesus' conduct or teaching, but how he reacts to His suffering and dying.

It almost seems as though the important thing about Jesus' life was not what He did, but what was done to Him. All the verbs that refer to His life are passive verbs. This is in sharp contrast to the verbs that follow—"descended," "rose again," "ascended," "sitteth," "shall come." These are all active. The Creed surely gives the very clear impression that it understood Christ's life in terms of the meaning of His death. He was laying down His life for the sheep. He had come into the world to give His life "a ransom for many."

Perhaps it is always true that if you want to know the meaning of a person's life, you will get the surest clue by inquiring for what and how he died. For what is a man willing to suffer, even at the risk of dying? "Arrested by the Gestapo"—that would tell you much about a man, even if it were all you knew about him. "Imprisoned by action of the People's Court of Hungary"—that gives you some insight into what Bishop Ordass stands for that makes it quite unnecessary for him to reply to self-styled defenders of the "American way."

"Suffered under Pontius Pilate" tells us a great deal about Jesus Christ, "God's only Son, our Lord." Here was one whose life came into conflict with the representative of Roman tyranny. Even though Rome did not take the initiative in putting Him away, having hardly taken any serious note of Him, Pontius Pilate became so inextricably enmeshed in the infamy of Jesus' death that Christian generations to the end of time will associate Christ's suffering with him. But it is extremely important to remember that Pilate acted with the wholehearted endorsement of the representatives of Jewish law and order, too. This is sufficient evidence that Jesus was not put to death for His opposition to Rome. Pilate stands not only as the representative of Roman law and order, but of all law and order, of all institutions of justice. Jesus suffered at the hands of men. He was crucified not by criminals but with criminals. Mark that difference carefully! It was not some lawless action by an enemy who eluded the agents of law and order that was responsible for His suffering and dying. It was precisely at the hands of those who had the power to enforce justice, to protect the innocent, and to punish the guilty, that Jesus met His death.

If you would understand what the coming of God into the world in the person of Jesus Christ means, you must reckon with the way He died. Law and order and justice were over on the side of those who destroyed the holy and righteous One. Therefore, it is not only a few lawless and wretched men who stand condemned by the Cross. All men and all that product of law and justice and culture which they have produced through the long sweep of the centuries, stands judged by the cross on which He suffered with the guilty—the malefactors who were crucified, one on His right and one on His left.

Undoubtedly, there was an important historical reason, too, for summarizing the life of Jesus in this way. From very early times there has been a heresy seeking to establish itself in the Christian community. Can God who is perfect in all respects really suffer? Is not suffering due to lack of power or wisdom? The recurring heresy has insisted that God cannot really suffer, for He lacks nothing. If, then, Jesus suffered, it must have been only in His human nature, in his role as man, and not in His divine nature. Therefore, His suffering is not really a matter of any consequence in the experience of God. The Creed emphatically rejects this heresy. He who is "God's only Son," who was "conceived by the Holy Ghost, born of the Virgin Mary"—He it is who "suffered under Pontius Pilate" and who now "sitteth on the right hand of God the Father Almighty."

For the Christian, God is perfect Love, and "love is patient and kind," love bears the burdens and takes the stripes that belong to another. This is His perfection and His glory.

WAS CRUCIFIED, DEAD, AND BURIED

TEXT: *Luke 23:50-56*

"CRUCIFIED, DEAD, AND BURIED"—these are somber words. We might be in the mood for them on Good Friday, if we have carefully and prayerfully prepared ourselves through a Lenten season. Yet, these are the words which we confess each Sunday, or as often as we confess the Apostles' Creed. They have reference to something very central in our Christian faith, and we must not slide over them too easily.

What they do have reference to has been suggested already: the key to Jesus' life is in His death. In the perspective of faith, even while we join in all the choruses of praise that exalt His life, the astonishing thing about Him is not so much how He lived, but how He died. In the experience of those who have been taken captive by Him, it has characteristically been "the word of the cross" that has been "the power of God unto salvation."

Madeline Caron Rock has called Him "the Wounded Greatness of the world." Worshiping congregations bow in adoration before that "Sacred Head now wounded, with grief and shame weighed down." One of the poets has expressed the feeling of many of us in these words,

O King, O Captain, wasted, wan with scourging,
Strong beyond strength and wonderful with woe,

Whither relentless wilt Thou still be urging
Thy lame and halt that have not strength to go?
Peace! Peace! I follow. Why must we love Thee so?[2]

There is a sort of madness and exaltation in the Cross. In every Lenten season a great company finds new resources for living by focusing its thought and attention on the dying Lord.

I have called attention to the fact that the Apostles' Creed passes over the life of Jesus with only this one reference, "Suffered under Pontius Pilate." As though to emphasize further the disparity between the emphasis upon His life and the emphasis upon His death, there are three statements about the latter.

"Crucified"—that is the way He died. This was the instrument which men used in their effort to rid themselves of God. Perhaps its principal significance is that the ancient world knew of no worse way to put a man to death. There was no one so bad that a worse penalty than crucifixion would have been meted out to him. The Assyrians may have invented crucifixion. The Romans are said to have crucified by the thousands. It was the worst death, the most degrading end, the most excruciating torture which the contemporaries of Jesus could have imposed upon Him.

Amos Wilder, one of our contemporary American poets, has pointed out at least one implication of this.

Therefore that One
Who most was man, shrank from the shame
Of any lot less shameful than another's,
Fearing the ignominy of a name
Less ignominious than some human brother's.

That none
Might claim before Him to know well
The tranced tortures of some deeper hell,

---

[2] Author not known.

Or cast reproachful glances from a fiercer cross,
Asking in vain for faith in some more hopeless loss,
And hope for some more desperate enterprise,
And love for some more utter sacrifice.[3]

Such was the identification of God's only Son with men in all their pain and shame.

"Dead"—when you have said that about a man you have written the last line, the last word. There is nothing more to be said. Death is the final enemy to which all men must yield. To die is to fall on the field of battle, and to yield the field to the conqueror. Death is the final despair of all who live on the assumption that "earth is enough." It is the final mockery for all of those who would "eat, drink, and be merry for tomorrow you die"—tomorrow you die!

We shall never be able to understand how it could be that He who was "God's only Son" could die, just as we shall never be able to understand how He could be born. But whether or not we understand it, we triumphantly confess that it was thus that He became our Lord. Such was His identification with men for whom it is appointed once to die, that death came to Him, too, as it must to all men. And it was by submitting to death that He conquered it for himself and for us all.

"Buried"—when that has been done, men have done all that they can do for him who has died. Then the whole drama is over, or at least the episode that involved this person who is no longer among the living. The story will have to be put together again, and life will have to go on, but without the one we have loved and lost.

And yet, even as we confess these words, we know that all is not over. Not, at least, when we are speaking about Jesus

---

[3] Quoted from G. Stewart, *The Crucifixion in Our Street* (New York: Doran, 1927) p. 49.

Christ. For He who had so utterly identified himself with men that He died their death was not to be death's choicest victim. He was to be the victor who would break the bonds of death. He had not identified himself with men in their shame in order that a new chapter in human infamy might be written, but that men might be saved from the deepest depths of shame. It was not to share man's tomb, but to shatter it, that He joined His human brothers in the "silent halls of death."

"Crucified, dead, and buried"—for all of us this is the end. For Him it was the place of triumph, the place of beginning again.

DESCENDED INTO HELL

TEXT: *1 Peter 3:18-20; Ephesians 6:10-12*

SOMETIMES ONE HEARS IT SAID that the creeds of the church are outdated, and need to be rewritten. We are told that they do not speak to the modern man and the modern world. Some branches of the Christian Church have tried to rewrite their creeds in order to make them more acceptable and more meaningful to the modern man. Whenever the argument for "modernizing" the creeds is advanced, one can be almost certain that the rubric, "descended into hell," is scheduled for deletion or radical revision.

Many people find this statement very difficult to accept, and they are apt to confess it with tongues in cheeks. It implies, we are told, a primitive three-story view of the universe, with hell below the earth and heaven above it, and this kind of universe has long since become an impossible one in the face of what we know about the world as it really exists. Besides, "hell" is an unpopular idea (although a popular enough word) which is supposed to reflect a primitive conception of God which we have outgrown in recent years.

It cannot be denied that our ways of thinking are quite different from those of the ancients, and it is surely true that it is more difficult for us than it was for them to understand what is intended by the phrase "descended into hell." But this is not because the ancients were so naive and materialistic in

82

their conceptions, but because we are. It is we who have to be able to locate hell in order to acknowledge its existence. It is we whose horizons do not extend beyond the temporal and the spatial. Secularism, the inability to think in other than this-worldly terms, is our disease more than it was theirs.

Try for a moment to move into the Biblical view of existence. We may be able to find a point from which this item in our Creed would be illumined. Take that passage out of Paul's letter to the Ephesians, for instance. The presupposition is that this life is a battleground. There are two kingdoms at war—the kingdom of God and the kingdom of evil; and we are involved in the warfare. We need to be armed for battle. But we do not fight other men—we fight against "the principalities, against the powers, against the world rulers of this darkness, against the spiritual hosts of wickedness in the heavenly places."

The good that there is in the world can never be explained without reference to a source of good outside of the good man. To be good is to be obedient to some law that is not of our own making; it is to be the instrument of a power larger than oneself. And the evil that is in the world is not a kind of independent evil. It is not merely the absence of goodness. In the Biblical view, evil in the world is the expression of a kingdom of evil that is governed by the evil one. It is the expression of intelligent will, often if not always more cunning and clever and calculating than goodness.

One has to understand what the church means by its confession that Jesus "descended into hell" against the background of this great cosmic conflict between good and evil, God and the devil. If one wants an analogy, any military conflict will provide it. The war in Korea, for instance, was not between groups of men engaged in fighting; not between armies, but between countries, both of them representative of combinations or alliances of nations. The outcome of the battle in Korea affected nearly every capitol in the world.

In the same way, this world is a battleground. Every life and every age is a battleground. It is being fought between God and all that is over against Him. The decisive event in this conflict which is as long as history itself, is the coming of God's "only Son" to engage the forces of evil in man's behalf and at his side. He changed the tide of battle on the field where the battle was being fought—on this earth, in human history. He did it in an entirely unexpected way. He allowed evil to concentrate and exhaust its powers upon Him and to destroy Him. He was "crucified, dead, and buried." But then He arose from the dead, and turned everything upside down again. It is this unexpected way of overcoming evil that is dramatized in some of the ancient views of how Christ had deceived the devil.

Now, what is the meaning of the confession, "He descended into hell"? It is the confident assertion that Christ won not only a battle, at one point in human history, where He himself engaged evil, but that He won the war. He defeated the whole kingdom of evil. He dethroned the devil. He won a cosmic victory. The whole universe was affected by that decisive triumph of Jesus Christ on the cross. There is no citadel of evil left untouched. There is no reason anymore why anyone should be overcome by evil. To serve the devil is to be the slave of a dethroned power. Rise up and claim your freedom! Only those are in bondage who do not know that they have been made free.

The devil has only two weapons with which he seeks to exercise his dominion over men. The one weapon is the suggestion that we are good enough as it is; we do not need to have a God come in to shield us from our sin. And that weapon has been broken by the devastating exposure of all human pretensions to goodness when the good men of the world crucified Christ with criminals—one on the right and one on the left. The other weapon is the argument that we are so bad that there is no hope for us. And that weapon has been shattered by that unbelievable love which could say of those who crucified Him, "Father, forgive them," and which could come back on Easter morning with no other message for the world than "the remission of sins."

The victory of God in Christ was complete. He conquered the capitol, the citadel of the kingdom of evil.

THE THIRD DAY HE ROSE AGAIN
FROM THE DEAD

TEXT: *Acts 2:22-36*

WE HAVE COME TO EASTER IN THE APOSTLES' CREED. In one sense, this is the starting point for the Christian faith. We understand the meaning of Christmas and Good Friday because we have come to know Easter. When we stand at the empty tomb, the suffering and the death look different from what they did before. There would be no glory about the suffering and the dying, if that were the end of it. Even to suffer innocently and patiently and to die nobly offers no hope for men, if this is the last word that can be spoken. Indeed, to know that the world crucified the noblest offspring of the race is ground for cynical despair, rather than for hope. If this is what happens to the best of men, what reason have we for believing that there is any justice in life, or that virtue and goodness have any chance of survival. The light that shines upon the suffering and the dying, and that makes the Cross the symbol of radiant and redeeming hope, is a light that comes from beyond the tomb.

The first disciples saw in the resurrection of Christ a reversal of the apparent meaning of the events which had preceded it. The passage from Peter's sermon on the day of Pentecost as well as most of the sermons in the Book of Acts bear witness to the central importance which the original disciples attached to this unbelievable, frightening, and redeeming reversal of the outcome. The obvious meaning of His suffering, death, and burial was that this One in whom they had come to believe as the Messiah was not the Messiah. "We had hoped that he was the one to redeem Israel," said the travelers along the Emmaus road. But now the worst in men had destroyed the best of men. They could carry with them the memory of One who deserved to triumph, but the facts of history were that He had not. Death is, humanly speaking, the ultimate defeat that can be suffered. There is no court of appeal that can change the verdict and reclaim the innocent after the death penalty has been executed. Death is so awfully final. There is every indication that the disciples accepted the finality of what had happened.

Easter was an utter surprise to them. The last thing that they had expected was that they would see Him alive again. He had talked to them about rising again from the dead, but they at least did not understand that this implied His return into their midst.

Easter had something frightening about it, too. While on the one hand it was too good to be true—they hardly dared believe it—on the other hand there is clear evidence that they were not entirely comfortable in His presence. How could it be otherwise! Not one of them could face Him without embarrassment. They had all been unworthy of Him in that night in which He was betrayed. And for those who had not been His friends but His enemies, the return of the risen Christ would be frightening indeed. Suppose it be true that the essential nature of God is justice and power, as is so generally assumed; that by some inner necessity of His own being, God must reward men for their little righteousnesses and punish them for their little misdeeds, and that His power is entirely ample to accomplish this. Would it not then follow that His return to the scene of history's greatest crime would have been a return in judgment? Who could have raised a voice in protest, if He had come with the thunder of judgment to vindicate God against men?

But Easter, with its reversal of the meaning of the events of the last week of Jesus' life, was redeeming, too. He to whom men had done their worst when they nailed Him to the tree, had done His best for men. He came back to claim unworthy disciples as His own, without a word of rebuke or censure. He gave them a gospel of forgiveness to be preached to all the world—to priest and scribe, to Pilate and Annas, Pharisees and publicans, friend and foe. The God who was incarnate in Jesus Christ is love. The incontrovertible proof of it is the death and resurrection of our Lord. It is this absolute and unconditioned love of God, which could take all the evil that there is in the world into itself and bear it in place of those who should have borne it—it is this that is the "good news." There is nothing that men can do to God that they did not do to Him when they nailed Jesus Christ to the cross; and He came back to forgive them. This is the rock foundation upon which our faith is fixed. He allowed sin to do to Him what it should have done to the evildoer. There is nothing that God can do for men which He did not do for them when He bore their sins in His body on the tree.

It may seem to you that I return to this theme with almost tiresome repetition, but I do so because it is what I understand to be the gospel, of which I have been made a minister. I hope that you will hear it so often and in so many ways through the entire program of this institution that you will never be able to forget it. Then you will understand what Christianity really means, you will have an anchor in the storms of life, and you will have a source of insight and power that will hold you firmly to the Christian "way."

There are two other implications of the resurrection of Christ which I want to suggest. The first is this: there is no use trying to find an explanation for the Resurrection that will make it easier to believe. It stands as the counterpart to the mystery of His birth. Jesus did not return to prove to Pilate or Annas or Caiaphas that He had triumphed over them. It was only to those who were willing to be His disciples that the evidence came. It is so still. He seems to be unwilling to bludgeon the minds of the unbelieving into submission, or to force their wills to a reluctant obedience.

The second implication has reference to the final end. You must have wondered sometimes how this long and often dreary battle against evil is going to come out. Is it a "tale told by an idiot, full of sound and fury, signifying nothing"? Does the last word lie with war and sickness and hatred and death? There is an answer to that in the resurrection of Christ. The last word does not lie with hatred and conflict, but with love and peace; not with death and the devil, but with life and God. The God who created our world for some purpose beyond our highest hope does not intend to fail. His is now and shall be forever "the kingdom and the power and the glory. Amen."

HE ASCENDED INTO HEAVEN

TEXT: *Acts 1:6-11*

THE CHRISTIAN CONFESSION OF FAITH in Christ's resurrection, in His ascension, and in His enthronement at God's right hand all testify to the unexpected triumph and exaltation of Christ. They express that strange, fearful, and saving reversal of what appeared to be the final defeat for Christ and all for which He stood. They are statements about what happened after men had done their worst—and God took over to do His best. What has already been said with regard to the Resurrection concerning the divine intervention into the story and the impossibility of "explaining" God's action, applies equally to all the remaining items in this article. Of course, in a sense it applies to everything that God does, but here especially we are dealing with something which cannot even be described. Each of these assertions of faith, however, has a particular contribution to make toward the Christian understanding of the "mighty acts of God" by which Christ was "raised up" and "exalted."

The Christian Church affirms its faith in the Ascension as a fact—as something that really happened. There is not too much about it in the Biblical record. Matthew makes no clear reference to it. It is recorded in a single verse in Mark, and this occurs in what some scholars regard as a later addition to the original work. John makes no mention of it. Luke gives the most complete account, both in the Gospel of Luke and in the Book of Acts. He identifies the place, and tells us that two angels appeared to the disciples as they beheld Him ascending, and said, "Men of Galilee, why do you stand looking into heaven? This Jesus who was taken up from you into heaven, will come in the same manner as you saw him go into heaven." While John does not describe the event, he does record the words of Jesus, "Do not hold me, for I have not yet ascended to the Father." Paul is familiar with the Ascension and makes reference to it, as does 1 Peter. There can be no doubt that it was part of the primitive Christian faith that He whom they had come to know as the Messiah, who was among them as a brother, and who had appeared to them after the Resurrection, had returned to heaven at a fixed point in time. There had come a day when they no longer expected Him to appear among them because they had witnessed His ascension to God's right hand.

But the Apostles' Creed is a confession of faith, rather than just an assertion of facts. We need to ask ourselves what it meant to that early church, and what it means to us today, that Jesus ascended into heaven.

What does it mean to believe that Jesus ascended into heaven? Well, it means that in whatever way Jesus had left heaven in order to come to earth, He had now left earth in order to return to heaven. He who was rich and for our sakes had become poor had now returned to the riches that were properly His. He who had existed in the form of God and had emptied himself, taking the form of a servant, had now been reinstated in all the glory and power which were His before the world began. He had not finally been impoverished by His entrance into our human history, or by having been the victim of man's evil deed. He had lost nothing by the fact that men had taken from Him everything!

It meant, too, that He was beyond the reach of the evil

that men might want to do to Him. For man's sake He had placed himself at the mercy of men, but He was at their mercy no longer. The battle that He had fought and won on Golgotha was a final and decisive battle. There can be no more Gethsemanes for Him, no more crucifixion, no more dying—for Christ has ascended into heaven. What had happened was final and forever. To be sure, there is a sense in which men can "crucify the Son of God on their own account and hold him up to contempt," but this is by virtue of what one does to the Lord who was once crucified. The issue of the battle can never be in doubt again, as it was then.

When one has said this, he must immediately say something else which seems to be at odds with it. The Christ who ascended did not shed His human history, or leave it behind Him. The Christ who ascended is and will always be the Christ who was born of the Virgin Mary, suffered under Pontius Pilate, was crucified, dead, and buried. God knows now, in a way that He did not know before, what it is like to be a man. He knows what it means to be tempted as we are. He has had the experience of growing from infancy to youth into manhood; He knows what it is like to be hungry, and tired, and loved, and scorned, lonely and forsaken. He knows what it is like to be a good man in an evil world. It isn't possible to find a parallel for God or for the Incarnation. The beggar who has become a man of wealth still knows from experience what it is like to be a beggar. A king, disguising himself as a peasant, may gain some experience of what it is like to be a subject in his own realm. But these are not really parallels. The beggar is almost certain to forget, once he becomes rich, and the disguised king is likely to remember too well that he is only disguised as a peasant. But the Ascension means that Christ will never forget. His manhood has been taken up into the being of God. It can never be said of the God who was made man for our salvation, that He doesn't know what you and I are up against. Therefore, He is able to succour us in all our temptations, and comfort us in all our affliction.

If we have spoken too confidently about the meaning of the Ascension, as though it were a simple matter, this will need to be corrected. We are touching here upon one of the perennial mysteries with which the Christian faith and thought have wrestled through the centuries. The mystery which is involved in the Incarnation is this: How could the divine God come to earth and be made man without surrendering His divinity? The mystery of the Ascension is this: How could He who had been man return to God without surrendering His humanity? The two mysteries are exactly equal, and both are confidently affirmed by the Christian Church.

One other observation should be made. When Jesus ascended into heaven, He did not leave the earth in the sense that He is no longer here. On the contrary, His ascension brought Him closer to us than He could ever have been to His own contemporaries. He left in order that He might be nearer to us all. "It is to your advantage that I go away," He said. Otherwise the "Comforter" could not come. He was taken away from among men in order that He might come to dwell within men. And He who has come to rule in our hearts and lives is the ascended Lord, the triumphant and conquering Christ. It is this that we here confidently affirm.

AND SITTETH AT THE RIGHT HAND
OF GOD THE FATHER ALMIGHTY

TEXT: *Mark 16:14-20*

THE EARLY CHRISTIANS were quite sure that was where the road finally led—from Bethlehem and Galilee and Good Friday and Easter and the Ascension, to God's right hand. Mark does not offer any proof for it; he simply states it as an affirmation of faith.

Neither does he offer any explanation of why it was important that He should be at God's right hand. It would not be necessary to do so for those who would read his words. They would know that the right side was the place of honor in which the most favored and most powerful member of the royal retinue would always be found. Whoever was at the right hand of the king had the ear of the king as no one else did, and was able to speak for the king as no one else could.

And the Christians were sure that was where Jesus Christ had gone. Some of them remembered how in that early morning when He seemed the pitiable victim before His judges He had said, with more confidence than the circumstances seemed to warrant, "But from now on the Son of Man shall be seated at the right hand of the power of God." And they knew now that He was right. The first martyr, Stephen by name, the victim of that same Sanhedrin, could say, "Behold, I see the heavens opened, and the Son of man standing at the right hand of God." Paul makes it a part of the triumphant song of victory with which the eighth chapter of Romans closes: "If God is for us, who is against us? He who did not spare His own Son but gave him up for us all, will he not also give us all things with Him? Who shall bring any charge against God's elect? It is God who justifies; who is to condemn? Is it Christ Jesus, who died, yes, who was raised from the dead, who is at the right hand of God, who indeed intercedes for us?" The writer of the Epistle to the Hebrews adds one jeweled phrase to another in praise of Christ—"the effulgence of his glory," the "very image of his substance,"' and then caps it all with the highest praise and the most complete ascription of Deity which he can make in relation to Christ by saying that He "sat down at the right hand of the Majesty on high."

Now what does this phrase really mean? Even for people who are not particularly alert to the figurative implications of Biblical language and rather unimaginative in our own use of religious terms, it must be apparent that we are not talking about a location. Whether Jesus occupies a chair at all, and if so, whether it is to the left or to the right of the Father's chair, is a matter of so little concern to the Christian that even the introduction of such a triviality almost seems a bit sacrilegious.

No, it means something else than location. You could put it this way: Jesus Christ defines for us the sovereign character of God, just as He defines the saving character of God. The God who rules the world is none other than the God who through Christ redeemed the world. If that seems unimportant, perhaps unintelligible, look at it again. The God who rules in nature and in history, the God who has left His footprints on the rocks and in the seas, the God of harvest and of hail, the God of the sunset and the thunder, the God who rules through policemen, governors, presidents, and kings, the God who exercises His dominion through laws and courts and penalties and prisons, through international tribunals and even in the clash and fall of nations and of empires, indeed even to the point where civilization fades and history ends—the God who rules in all of this is a God who is like Jesus Christ. Indeed, He is so like Him that there isn't any point in distinguishing between them. It is Jesus Christ who sits in the place of dominion "at God's right hand."

Do you really believe that? It is so easy to believe that there are two Gods; one who is stern and just and demanding, who rules with a rod of iron, and one who is soft and approachable and forgiving. Between them there seems to be some kind of understanding that makes the world manageable. The one God maintains order in the world by the exercise of His power, and the other God redeems individuals by the exercise of His love. But it is not that way at all; right there at the right hand of God's power sits Jesus Christ.

There are tremendous implications in this common Christian affirmation about the place of Christ in the power of God. It has implications for our understanding of nature and of history. Whatever can rightly be attributed to God, directly or indirectly, must have some loving purpose in it like that which led Jesus to the cross. It has implications for social and political ethics. Everyone who exercises authority in the world needs to know to what kind of Sovereign he is obligated. We do not serve an abstract justice or static order. We serve a God whose fullest revelation of himself is in forgiveness and redemption.

Have you the audacity and the courage to believe that the God to whom you are answerable in all the relationships of your lives, indeed the only God there is, is the God who was in Jesus Christ reconciling the world to himself? It's a daring thing to believe!

FROM THENCE HE SHALL COME TO
JUDGE THE QUICK AND THE DEAD

TEXT: *Matthew 23:35-44*

WE HAVE NOW REACHED THE FINAL ITEM in the Second Article of the Creed. In one sense it affirms what has already been asserted about the exaltation to God's "right hand." The final and authoritative voice belongs to Jesus Christ. We have already seen that this is true as far as God is concerned. Therefore He is seated at God's right hand. But now we confess that He occupies the place of dominion at our right hand as well. He has the final and authoritative word with regard to us. He will come to judge the living and the dead.

An important difference must be noted, however. The authority and power which the Son exercises at the Father's right hand rests upon the unity of mind and will and character between the Father and the Son. They agree. But the power and authority of the Son over us does not rest on any such agreement between Him and us. We are not at one with God in mind and will and character. Our ways are not God's ways, nor are our thoughts His thoughts. Therefore, the Christ who sits at the right hand of every man is a judge, and His final and authoritative word is a judgment upon us all.

Let us see whether we cannot bring this a little closer to each of us. Suppose that you were given until sunset today

97

to settle all your accounts. Suppose, further, that you could gather together all the people with whom you had an account to settle into this room. There would be the people to whom you owed money, or who owed money to you; there would be all the ones against whom you have grievances or who have grievances against you; those for whom you should have done something that you have not done, or to whom you should not have done something that you have done. I'm sure that we would quickly agree that this room would not be large enough to hold them all for any one of us. And then suppose you settled every account, and one by one the folks would leave until the last of them was gone. When the last of them was gone, would you then be alone? No, you would never be alone. There would be one left. Even though you stayed all night, all week, all year, all your life—He would never leave. You would leave first. There would be an account to be settled, but it would not be your account with Him; it would be His account with you. And this One who would never leave the room would be Jesus Christ, seated "at the right hand of God the Father Almighty; from thence he shall come to judge the quick and the dead."

His presence there to the very end wouldn't depend at all on whether you wanted Him to be there or not, or whether you were on His side or not. In fact, it wouldn't depend on anything—not even your knowing that He was there, or thinking that He wasn't.

And what would be the account which He has to settle with you? Well, it might very well include how you had settled your accounts with the others. But even if you had settled all of them honestly and fairly you wouldn't get rid of Him or avoid the account which He has to settle with you. He might put it this way, as He did once to the twelve disciples, "What do you think of the Christ? Whose son is he?" The decisive and crucial matter for all of us is how we stand in relation to Jesus Christ; are we His willing and obedient subjects, or are we aligned with the rebels against Him? If we are His disciples, our future is as sure as His triumph over sin and death and hell. If we are aligned with Him, the fact that He is the final judge is our sure hope; if we are aligned against Him, it is our sure despair.

We have been speaking about individuals in the presence of Him who is to come to judge the quick and the dead. At every point Christianity is intensely personal. No one can escape from the judgment by taking refuge in the mob. But Christianity is cosmic and universal, too. What has been said about us as individuals can be said about all of us together. And not only about all of our contemporaries but also about all who ever have lived or ever will live. All are finally under the judgment of Christ. When tomorrow has become yesterday, and all the future has become history; when the last account has been settled, the last battle fought, and the last victory won; when God's fair earth has been turned into charred cinders, if that is to be its fate; when the clock of time has finally run down, however it is to happen—there at the end will be the Son of Man coming on the clouds of glory to judge the world. The unsettled account at the end of it all will be His account with the world. At the last humanity must answer, the living and the dead, for what they have done with what He gave them.

The Christian Church has never yielded—at least not until very modern times—to the temptation to be overly optimistic about what could be accomplished here on earth. It has usually safeguarded itself carefully against the assumption that earth would gradually improve until it would become heaven, or that men would improve in it so that the transfer from earth to heaven would be a very ordinary thing. At the end of history, when human possibilities have been exhausted, or time has run out, the fulfillment of God's purposes for men calls for so radical a transformation that from the side of men it will look like "the end of the world." But from God's point of view, and from the point of view of the redeemed, it means "a new heaven and a new earth," which is distinguished most of all from this one by the fact that in it "righteousness dwells."

On the other hand, the church has been equally emphatic that Christians must avoid the conclusion that since earth cannot be transformed into heaven by human efforts, all human effort is futile. We are to be judged by Him who is also the Lord of life, and who does not overlook even the cup of cold water given in His name. This moment and every moment to the end of time, God will be waiting to settle His account with us; and the God who will always be standing there to judge us and our efforts is the God who died on a cross, arose from a borrowed tomb, ascended into heaven, sat down at the right hand of God, whence "He shall come to judge the quick and the dead."

I BELIEVE IN THE HOLY GHOST

TEXT: *John 16:1-15*

THE CHURCH CONFESSES that it believes in a Trinity—
Father, Son, and Holy Ghost. It is usually suggested by those
who do not share this faith, that the "doctrine of the Trinity"
has needlessly complicated the whole matter, and is probably
intended only for such professional theologians as can afford
to speculate about utterly meaningless things. On the other
hand, it has been argued very impressively that if the only
thing one could say about God was that He is one, then God
would be entirely beyond all our thinking or talking. Unity is
more of an abstraction than trinity. There is no way of saying less about anything than to say that it is "one"—"a" something. As soon as one says anything about it, he begins to
name its parts or its qualities or its relationships. If you should
care to pursue that line of thought any further, I would suggest you consult Hodgson, *The Doctrine of the Trinity.*

Whatever might have been the possibility of knowing God
in other ways—as one or many—it is sufficient for our purposes
to recognize that we do actually know Him as Father, Son,
and Holy Ghost. We know Him as the Father Almighty,
maker of heaven and earth—the God whose power and majesty
accounts for all existence, who stands before and behind the
created world. We know Him as Jesus Christ, His only Son,
Our Lord—the God who is revealed and disclosed in human

J. E. MOREN

form, a brother of all men, through whom we have come to know that God is love because through Jesus Christ we have become the beneficiaries of His love and grace. We know Him as the Holy Ghost—the God who confronts every generation and every man as a contemporary, and who will take up His abode within us, if we let Him. These are not three Gods but only one. The God who confronts us now as the Holy Ghost is none other than the God who created the world and who became flesh and dwelt among us in Jesus Christ. In terms of the ancient Nicene Creed, the Holy Ghost "proceedeth from the Father and the Son." He is the Spirit of God and has made His way into the world and into human hearts through Jesus Christ.

One might say that we are speaking about three points of view from which one may think of God. First, from the point of view of His dependent creatures. He is our Creator and Sustainer. Second, from the point of view of forgiven sinners. He is our Savior and Lord. Third, from the point of view of the fellowship and the struggle into which one enters through the forgiveness of sins. He is the constant Presence who "calls, gathers, enlightens, and sanctifies the whole Christian Church on earth." But even if we are helped to see what the Trinity means by these three points of view, we must not conclude that they are only points of view, and that God is finally only one after all. We would not accurately reflect the faith of the church if we did not insist that it is really God that we have come to know in each of these three ways. We have no surer knowledge of God than that which has come to us through the gospel and which we have received in this way. We must not allow anyone, however bright he may seem to be or claim to be, to go behind this revelation of God as Father, Son, and Holy Ghost, and put it all together again for us, so that we could say all that we would want to say about God without talking about a Trinity.

In one way, our confession of faith in the Holy Ghost is rather hard to account for. It would be wrong to suppose that the disciples had a doctrine of the Holy Ghost firmly fixed in their minds when Christ died, or even when He arose again and ascended into heaven. Something happened at Pentecost that seems to have been of decisive importance, but it was not quite as simple as it may sound at this distance. You remember that the Apostle Paul encountered Christians years later in Ephesus who had not even heard of the Holy Ghost. To be sure, they had been baptized in the baptism of John but they are considered by the writer of Acts to have been disciples of the new Way. No one set out to construct a doctrine of the Holy Ghost. They found themselves driven to it by the nature of the fellowship into which they had come through Jesus Christ.

There seem to me to be three reasons at least why this happened. First of all, they could not talk about the intimate nearness of God to each of them without talking about God in terms of the Holy Ghost. God, the Father Almighty, may be and often has been conceived to be far removed from the world that He brought into being. God the Son was close to His contemporaries—He was in very truth one of them. But He died, and while to be sure He rose again, and they felt and knew His presence among them for a little while, they also knew that He had ascended into heaven, and had sat down at the right hand of God the Father Almighty, whence He would come to judge the quick and the dead. And in the meantime? Was He not still among them? God had not moved farther away because Jesus had returned to His right hand. He was in fact closer to them than He had ever been before. This continuing nearness the doctrine of the Holy Ghost affirms.

A second reason that the Christians had to talk in terms of the Holy Ghost was their recognition that God was active and powerful in their midst, not merely as one who stood above them as a mighty Sovereign, nor as one who was among them as He had been in the days of Jesus' ministry, but also as one who was within them. The dominion of God that had been established in their lives was not like the dominion of law or coercive power, compelling them from without. It was not even the power of an example, the pull of a noble life that had been among them. God was ruling them from within, like a great loyalty, a great ideal, a great love. He had conquered their wills and made them His willing disciples. They found themselves on His side, informed by His truth and inspired and empowered by His Spirit. It had come to pass as He had said to them during that dark final week of His life: "It is to your advantage that I go away." It was necessary that He be taken away from among them in order that He might come to be within them. It is to this that the church bears witness when it confesses its faith in the Holy Ghost.

The third reason that Christians had to come to believe in the Trinity is that they had to recognize the dynamic and creative character of God's presence within them. Those in whom this power of God was at work "both to will and to do" were bold, inventive, daring, fearless, explosive. It wasn't long before they were talking about that little company of God-possessed people as those "who turn the world upside down."

The God who laid the foundations of the universe and determined its structure is a God of law and order and discipline. That aspect of God, the church affirms in its First Article. The God who came to us in Jesus Christ is a God of infinite compassion, boundless love, and in all respects the full revelation of the character that is divine. In a very profound sense this article of the Creed is the very center of our Christian faith. But it would be no adequate understanding of our commitment as Christians to conclude that our task is to reduplicate or imitate the life of Christ in ourselves, even if it were possible for us to do so. We are called to be ourselves— the selves God intended us to be. And this can happen only if we allow God to have His way with us, as Jesus did. Because Jesus lived and died and rose again this is not an altogether futile hope or empty dream. The Holy Ghost takes of the things of Christ and declares them unto us. Jesus himself promised that the Holy Ghost would lead us into all truth.

The doctrine of the Holy Ghost has more relevance to the issues of our time than most modern men suspect. You cannot go around making men fit into the molds that we think suit our time. The Holy Ghost is at work in every believer, and He is not to be regimented. You must not harness any generation completely to those that have preceded it. What is new may be of God, for God is at work in the world of men. He is at work, making men free.

THE HOLY CHRISTIAN CHURCH
THE COMMUNION OF SAINTS

TEXT: *Ephesians 1:15-23*

IT WAS THUS THE EARLY CHRISTIANS THOUGHT of themselves—as "the communion of saints." You do not find it in the writings of the New Testament itself, but by the time the Apostles' Creed came into existence it must have been a common and accepted definition. If it were not already in the Creed, I am not sure that we would put it there. For one thing, we have grown a bit squeamish about the word "saints." Most of us would probably disown the appelation. In our common speech it has come to mean one who makes a profession of exceptional piety and goodness, with at least a hint that this judgment might not be shared by others.

But, of course, this is not what the term means—not in its Biblical usage. And since it is a Biblical word, and we are talking about a Biblical idea, we should allow it to retain its own meaning. When Paul addressed a letter to the Corinthians in which he had some very harsh things to say about the level of piety and morality, he was not prevented from addressing them as "saints." This was his characteristic form of address in almost all of his letters, and there were few churches that escaped words of censure as well as of praise. All who heard the gospel were "called to be saints." They were those who "in every place call on the name of our Lord Jesus Christ, both their Lord and ours." They were those who had accepted Jesus Christ as their Lord, who lived by forgiveness, and who wanted to be identified with Him.

Between them there was a "communion." There was a fellowship which they had with one another because they had fellowship with Christ. Those who were on the outside sensed something unusual about that fellowship. "Behold how they love one another," they said. To be sure, there were factions and dissensions even in the Early Church, as Paul's letters amply testify; but there was still a fellowship that existed between those who were followers of Christ which did not exist among others or between others and themselves.

Paul often used the figure of the body. He spoke of the church as "the body of Christ." Christ was the head and they were the members. They were united by the fact that they had the same Lord, the same Spirit, the same God and Father of all. They had one faith, one baptism, one hope. There were diversities of gifts and diversities of services, but they were still "one body in Christ." It is probable that this was more than a figure of speech for Paul. He meant it quite literally. There had been a body in which Christ had walked among men, but that body was no longer on the earth. But Christ had not left the world in the sense that He was no longer present in it. They knew Him as an indwelling presence. The gospel which they proclaimed was His gospel; there was a power at work within them which was the power of His Spirit. They were His voice, His hands and His feet. The mighty movement of God's grace and power which had been in Christ and which had raised Him from the dead was now in them, taking captive the minds and hearts of men. As they proclaimed the "good news," others came into that fellowship which they had with Christ, and they knew that it was the Lord who was adding to them "day by day those that were being saved." A recent writer has put it this way: "The church is the form in which Christ since the Resurrection is present and confronts us here on earth."[4]

If one asks what the essential and decisive element in the church is—that without which it would not be the church—he will come upon three answers that have been given in Christendom. Some will say that it is faith in the hearts and minds of believers. The church is an association of people who think alike about Christ and who are committed to Him. And this answer is not wholly wrong. There would be no church if there were no believers. But, on the other hand, it is not the faith of the believers which creates the church, for faith cannot be caught like a sort of contagion. Another answer is that it is the priesthood, the ministry, which is the essential and constitutive element in the church. This is the view held by "hierarchical" churches. When this is asserted, it usually implies that there is a sort of authority residing in the hierarchy which has been handed down from the Apostles. This "apostolic succession" represents the continuing community of believers. And the third answer is that it is the Word of God, the gospel, which is the essential element in the church. Only the gospel has the power to produce faith in those who hear. Without the gospel the ministry would be futile. Without the gospel there would be no believing community. It is because this Word of God is present among us and is offered to us, as proclamation and as sacrament, that we are enabled to believe.

If the church is really the "communion of saints," it must be a matter of great concern to us that it is broken and divided into many different denominations and churches. Is this not a sort of violation of the body of Christ? We have one Lord, one Head—why should we not also be one body? It cannot be denied that our witness to Christ has been weakened

---

[4] A. Nygren, *En bok om kyrkan* (Lund: Svenska kyrkans diakonistyrelses bokförlag, 1943) p. 20.

by the fact that we cannot speak with one voice. But it must also be remembered that many of these divisions have grown out of an honest desire to be faithful to the gospel, to release it from human accretions that have attached themselves to an institution which is a human institution, even though it is the habitation of Christ in our world and time. Some divisions have resulted from the desire to bring out more clearly some neglected truth. Perhaps it is not so much the existence of many churches calling upon the same Lord which is the scandal, as it is our slowness in recognizing one another as members of the only church there is, the Church of Christ. In recent years we have come to acknowledge one another more willingly, and to form some bonds of fellowship which bear witness to the unity that we have in Christ. It is not too soon. For we must never treat Christ's Church as though it were our own.

THE FORGIVENESS OF SINS

TEXT: *Ephesians 1:3-10*

MOST CATECHISMS DISTINGUISH BETWEEN the Second and Third Articles of the Creed by saying that the Second deals with "Justification" and the Third with "Sanctification." Neither of the words is particularly familiar to contemporary student generations, but such cursory acquaintance as you may have with the words would undoubtedly suggest that "the forgiveness of sins" belongs with justification rather than with sanctification. For justification describes the action of God by which we are brought into fellowship with Him—and this clearly involves forgiveness. Sanctification has reference to becoming good, overcoming sin, and growing toward Christian maturity. To most of us this seems to be a more substantial sort of goodness than that which comes from forgiveness. Indeed, is not forgiveness a sort of substitute for goodness?

But here is "the forgiveness of sins," right in the center of the Third Article. When the church summed up what it had learned about the work of the Holy Ghost in human hearts, it put forgiveness at the center. One might have expected something else: like "regeneration," "conversion," "the new law of love," or "the kingdom of God." Any one of them would have been true, but they would not have represented the basic faith of the Christian Church concerning the work of the Holy Ghost. The central and essential thing that the church has learned from Christ about God is that He freely forgives sins for Jesus' sake. Luther says, "From this article there can be no budging or slacking, though heaven fall and earth and all else besides."

As has been pointed out previously, it is difficult for us fully to appreciate the gospel of forgiveness because we have such a shallow view of sin. We think of it as the violation of social standards or "mores." Perhaps a really serious sin may even be as bad as a crime. But this is not a religious sense of sin, certainly not a specifically Christian one. Sin is not merely violation of law; it is rebellion against the Lawgiver. It is the revolt of the creature against the Creator, and therefore against the laws of his own nature. Perhaps the closest human parallel would be the sense of unworthiness one feels when one has betrayed or disappointed a loved one; although that cannot be a real parallel because it has taken place between equals. The guilt which the sinner experiences over against God is always an absolute guilt, not balanced by any failures on His side, nor even affected by the sum total of human delinquency.

Like every serious malady that afflicts man, sin has attracted a multitude of "quack remedies." Their mark is always that they seek to cure by dealing with symptoms instead of with causes. For instance, there is the advice of the worldly wise to the sensitive soul—"forget it!" Time heals the wounds. It may have been a mistake, but there is no use getting morbid about it. If there are physical reminders, they can be drugged to silence.

And there is the almost automatic human response, to hide one's sin—even deny its existence. Or, we rationalize it and justify it. There were "mitigating circumstances." We said an awfully unkind thing to someone, but "he had it coming." Then, of course, we have to prove our case and scrutinize every action of his to find supporting evidence. It can always be found, if one is looking for it. Progressively one can be alienated from his friends and neighbors; he can come to live in an atmosphere of suspicion and hatred that warps and twists his soul as well as all his human relationships.

All of these "quack remedies" really assume that the sense of guilt is an illusion, that sin is only a notion. Will cancer yield to the cure of forgetfulness or secrecy or rationalization? Will ignorance be cured by hiding it? Will war or any other real problem in the world surrender its force before any of this subterfuge which we erect around our sin? Is death conquered by ignoring it?

Sin is a reality and it requires a real remedy. Sin is alienation from God and from fellow men. It tears apart the social body, because it is a distortion and perversion of the right relationship between the creature and the Creator. It is violation of the laws of our own existence, for we were created for fellowship both with God and our fellow men.

Forgiveness is a real remedy for a real ailment. Sin alienates; forgiveness reconciles. There can be no other basis for reconciliation between sinners than that of forgiveness. There can be no real fellowship between unforgiving friends. And there can be no real fellowship between God and men, unless forgiveness becomes the basis. "If we say we have no sin, we deceive ourselves, and the truth is not in us. If we confess our sins, he is faithful and just, and will forgive our sins and cleanse us from all unrighteousness." This is the meaning of the gospel, as Paul summarizes it, "In him we have redemption through his blood, the forgiveness of our trespasses, according to the riches of his grace which he lavished upon us." Because of Christ's life and death and resurrection, we can be assured of God's forgiving grace. Therefore, we may now have "fellowship one with another, and the blood of Jesus his Son cleanses us from all sin."

Psychologically, as well as theologically, only the forgiveness of God is adequate to release us from the burden of guilt. Until we hear the word of forgiveness spoken with the voice of God, there will be some uncertainty about it. When the Son makes us free, then we are free indeed. It is God working within us that enables us to see in Christ the ground and assurance of our forgiveness. Therefore, "the forgiveness of sins" stands in the center of our faith in the Holy Ghost.

But it must also be clear that living by forgiveness also means having the forgiving spirit. We cannot have the one without the other. "For if you forgive men their trespasses, your heavenly Father also will forgive you; but if you do not forgive men their trespasses, neither will your Father forgive your trespasses."

You might put it this way: forgiveness is at the center of our Creed because it is at the center of our lives. Be sure you keep it there!

THE RESURRECTION OF THE BODY

TEXT: *1 Corinthians 15:35-50*

JUST AS "FORGIVENESS" is the word which describes the work of the Holy Ghost today, so "resurrection" is the word which describes the work of the Holy Ghost for the future. It asserts that the work of the Spirit will be effective. We have now an "earnest of our inheritance," or, as the Revised Standard Version has it, "a guarantee of our inheritance until we acquire possession of it." But we look forward to the fullness of our inheritance. "For now we see in a mirror dimly, but then face to face. Now I know in part; then I shall understand fully, even as I have been fully understood." For we have been "born anew to a living hope through the resurrection of Jesus Christ from the dead," and we look forward to "an inheritance which is imperishable, undefiled, and unfading, kept in heaven" for us. "Our commonwealth is in heaven, and from it we await a Savior, the Lord Jesus Christ, who will change our lowly body to be like his glorious body, by the power which enables him even to subject all things to himself."

Let us look at this doctrine of "resurrection" and, specifically, "the resurrection of the body." It may be granted that there is some obscurity as to whether the Creed literally refers to the "body" or to the "dead." Some translations of the Creed hold to the latter. I doubt whether any serious problem can arise at this point. The emphasis lies on "resurrection," and this properly contrasts with the idea of immortality. Immortality, which has its origins in Greek thought, has reference to something in man which is not mortal and which consequently does not die. But within the Biblical concept of man, mortality is taken seriously. Man is mortal. There is nothing about him that goes on indefinitely, so to speak, by its own momentum. The resurrection is a creative act of God, and the affirmation of the Christian's faith in the resurrection is also an assertion of man's complete dependence upon God at the point of death. One does not escape from God by dying—this is precisely the point at which all escape is impossible. The only existence he has after death is the existence which God gives him through the resurrection from the dead. This applies alike to those who are for God and those who are against Him.

There is undoubtedly an obstacle for the modern man at this point. The "resurrection of the body" seems to be at odds with even an elemental knowledge of what happens to "earthly remains" when they are returned to the dust. The doctrine has seemed to many people to imply a kind of reassembling of molecules which is difficult to envisage and quite meaningless. Perhaps there have been times when something like this was the common understanding of the doctrine, but surely it was not in Paul's mind. He clearly distinguishes between the grain of wheat that is sown and the harvest that comes from it, between physical and spiritual, celestial and terrestrial glory, between "the image of the man of the dust" and the "image of the man of heaven."

There are at least three assertions contained in this doctrine which I should like to have you think of.

1) The "resurrection of the body" asserts the eternal significance of individual personality. It means that we continue as persons in that other world. How would you distinguish

between "disembodied spirits"? It is no accident that the idea of immortality becomes impersonal and abstract. You cannot conceive of individual personality without a body.

2) It asserts our faith that we shall eternally function in a society of individuals. The body is not the prison within which the person or "the soul" must function. It is the instrument by which it functions. The body is not so many pounds avoirdupois—it is sight, hearing, action, emotion, memory, mind, and whatever else has its seat and source in the body. How would disembodied spirits serve one another? The Christian faith affirms that love will have as adequate instruments with which to function in the world beyond as it has here.

3) The doctrine of the resurrection of the body asserts that our historical existence has eternal significance. The doctrine of immortality assumes that there is something indestructible in man—something by its very nature eternal, unaffected by change, or choice, or death. The doctrine of the resurrection of the body denies that there is anything by nature eternal in man, but, on the other hand, it asserts that there is nothing about man that can be sloughed off and left behind in the resurrection. There is nothing about man that ever really dies, in the sense that it no longer has relevance for him. The resurrection of the body is, in a sense, the resurrection of our history, too. We stand before God in the resurrection with the complete story of our lives written into our very persons. We are all that we have been. And the decisive thing, of course, will be whether we have the forgiveness of sins as a part of this history which we bring bodily to Him.

You see how the doctrine of the resurrection of the body is one of the great affirmations of the Christian faith! You can move out from this point to encompass all of human history and all of time within the doctrine. Nothing that we ever do as individuals, and nothing that we ever do collectively, can be unimportant any more. I could confess that there was a time when this doctrine seemed to me unimportant, if not misleading. Increasingly, it seems to me, it comes to encompass a whole Christian view of life and history within it.

For those who have known the healing of the word of forgiveness, the doctrine of the resurrection of the body becomes unbelievably good news. It means the triumph of Christ complete; it means the vanquishing of every foe, and the full glory which shall be revealed to us at the last day. We should say it with the voice of triumph! Let us not voice it meekly, as though we were afraid some chemist might prove us wrong.

THE LIFE EVERLASTING

TEXT: *John 17:1-3; Romans 6:22, 23*

WE HAVE CONTRASTED the idea of the "immortality of the soul" and the idea of the "resurrection of the body," and have said that the former is at home in Greek ways of thinking while the latter is distinctively Christian. Resurrection is God's creative intrusion into the fact of death. There is no human residue of soul or spirit which can be conceived of as continuing on by virtue of its own indestructibility. But there is "resurrection" for all, and this includes our total persons, all that we are.

There is a resurrection unto life and there is a resurrection unto judgment. You have it described for you in matchless power in the parable of the final judgment recorded in Matthew 25:31-46. Scarcely anything can be added to it, nor does anything need to be added. It does not need to be explained; it only needs to be read and pondered.

It may be worth noting that the Creed does not speculate concerning those who reject the gospel. For instance, we make no confession concerning what happened to those who crucified Christ, or concerning those who do not accept the forgiveness of sins. Similarly, we make no confession concerning those who do not inherit everlasting life. This is not to say that the Bible does not speak quite specifically to the point, but it is not a part of the Apostles' Creed. The Creed is a

118

positive affirmation throughout. This is properly the attitude
of the "believer." He is not called upon to pass judgment upon
others. It is enough to recognize that they with us will stand
before "the blessed and only Sovereign, the King of kings and
Lord of lords, who alone has immortality and dwells in unapproachable light."

It may be well to note, too, that the more recent translations of the Bible have substituted the word "eternal" for
most of the passages in which the Authorized Version used the
word "everlasting." This would seem to indicate the inade-
quacy of the thought of "unendingness" for that in which the
Christian here affirms his faith. It is quality as well as quantity. When Jesus can say, "This is eternal life, that they know
thee the only true God, and Jesus Christ whom thou hast
sent," it is apparent that He is not talking about just extension
in time. Eternal life is a present possession and has as its heart
and center, fellowship with God through Jesus Christ. Because it is fellowship with Him, it has reality both here and
hereafter. The life of the believer is linked with the Lord of
life and death; our lives are "hid with Christ in God." It is
as impossible to think of the believer's life with Christ ending
as it is to think of Christ himself ceasing to be.

Surely there can be no analogies from this earth which can
be transferred to that other world. "What no eye has seen,
nor ear heard, nor the heart of man conceived," God has prepared for those who love Him. "Now we see in a mirror
dimly, but then face to face." And yet we must speak in human language or remain silent.

When the Book of Revelation speaks of it, it puts in the
center the great white throne, and all around are the worshiping hosts. For the mark of that kingdom is obedience to
the divine Will. "He will dwell with them, and they shall
be his people." He that sits on the throne is the Lamb, and
they "serve him day and night in his temple." And still "they

rest from their labors," for love rests when it serves the object of its love. And they sing a new song, the song of the redeemed. He will "wipe away every tear from their eyes, and death shall be no more, neither shall there be mourning nor crying nor pain any more, for the former things have passed away."

We do well to read the Book of Revelation as we view a work of art or read a book of poetry. It takes more imagination than most of us can muster to read it as intelligently and appreciatively as the first readers did. It takes some study, too, for many of the allusions are entirely unfamiliar to us. But at least we can sense the majestic sweep of it, the grandeur of its view of the final outcome of the struggle in which we are all engaged. The clear answer that speaks out of it is that the Christ who died and rose again is the final arbiter of history. His is the last word, and the last word is Life—Life everlasting.

There is one additional observation which I should like to make. Although it is the clear teaching of Scripture that we are saved by faith in Christ, or by grace through faith, there are also passages that assert the place of works in the life to come. The judgment scene in Matthew 25, where our treatment of the sick, the poor, and the imprisoned is called to witness, is not without relevance at this point, even though those who had works to their credit were unconscious of it. Revelation 14:13 says of the "dead who die in the Lord," that "their deeds follow them." Perhaps we may put it this way: In the world to come we begin where we left off. Even the grave works no miracle. Deathbed conversions do not recover wasted lives. Here what was said with regard to one of the implications of "the resurrection of the body" fits into our faith in "the life everlasting." Even if we could be sure that we would grasp some future opportunity to switch to the side of the truimphant Lord, we would be the losers. Miss no opportunity to grow up into the stature of the full-grown man of God. You will still be far from the goal.

Of course, there are many unanswered questions that cluster around the life to come. But it is sufficient for me that God rules there according to His good and gracious will. For Him to have His way, that is heaven indeed.

PART THREE

The
Lord's Prayer

OUR FATHER WHO ART IN HEAVEN

TEXT: *Matthew 6:7-15*

WATCH YOUR PERSONAL PRONOUNS! There are times when only the first person singular will do. Sometimes it is more comfortable to say "We" when we should say "I." It is easier, for instance, to say, "We are a sinful people," than it is to say, "I have sinned against heaven and before you; I am no longer worthy to be called your son." But this is likely to be evading the real issue and seeking to shed responsibility by sharing it.

But there are other times when the pronouns should be plural. One of them is when we pray. At least, so Jesus thought, for He taught His disciples to pray saying, "Our Father," "Give us . . . our daily bread," "Forgive us our trespasses," "Lead us not . . . ," "Deliver us . . ." Prayer is never a private affair, even when we pray in secret and alone. No prayer is complete that does not include others.

Of course, we can and should pray for our most intimate and personal needs. We would be lacking in earnestness and sincerity, if we did not bring them to Him. But the God to whom we pray is not our private God; He is the God and Father of us all. If we did not also bring the needs of others to Him, and if we did not acknowledge that He is also and equally concerned about them, prayer could become a very selfish thing. Perhaps it often does.

124

For to think of God as a sort of personal bank account on whom or on which we can draw for added resources to enable us to do the things we want to do, is the most persistent and serious temptation that is likely to plague the pray-er. Prayer is not intended to be a means by which we subdue and convince a reluctant God, so that He does our bidding. Prayer is intended to subdue us, our wills and desires, so that God may have His way with us and through us. It will help us to remember that, if we pray, "Our Father who art in heaven."

So, when you pray, think of others. Your family, your friends, your associates, to be sure. But think also of the needy, the forgotten, the sick, the dying, the wayward, the wicked, the impoverished and underprivileged of the earth. Let your thoughts range far and wide, as you speak that word "Our Father . . ." And then pray for your own needs, too.

Jesus invited us to think of Him to whom we direct our prayers as our "Father." I suppose one could say that this was almost a major note in all Jesus' teaching. It was thus He thought of God. He came to bear witness to the Father. "No one has ever seen God; the only Son, who is in the bosom of the Father, he has made him known." "I and the Father are one." "He who has seen me has seen the Father."

Sometimes it may be hard for us to believe in the goodness of God; in sorrow and misfortune, in the face of great problems, in the midst of evil forces. But then, especially, we must remember to pray, saying, "Our Father," even if we have to add, "I believe, help my unbelief!" Sometimes, perhaps often, prayer is a battleground, and the battle is half won when we call Him, "Father."

Often we speak of the problems of prayer. Many have written on it, some of them in learned ways. None of us is likely to escape them wholly. Can prayer actually change anything? Is it merely a sort of auto-suggestion, giving us self-confidence, so that we harness our own resources for the task at hand? Is not the universe ruled by law, and could God intervene in it even if He wanted to? And why should He want to, in response to our private petition, when He has so many others to take into account, and when He has himself ordained the laws by which the universe operates? You can add to that number, beyond a doubt.

You are not likely to find satisfactory answers to all of them. There are so many places where it is the part of wisdom to recognize the limits of our wisdom. But it will help if we can remember that we pray to the Father "who is in heaven." We have already confessed in the First Article of the Creed that we believe in "God the Father Almighty, Maker of heaven and earth." Read some of the doxologies which Christians have addressed to Him in confident faith; like this one out of Paul's letter to Timothy, ". . . the blessed and only Sovereign, the King of kings and Lord of lords, who alone has immortality and dwells in unapproachable light, whom no man has ever seen or can see. To him be honor and eternal dominion. Amen." Or this one, out of the Revelation of St. John, "Great and wonderful are thy deeds, O Lord God the Almighty! Just and true are thy ways, O King of the ages! Who shall not fear and glorify thy name, O Lord?"

It is to Him that we pray! He is not a prisoner within His universe. He is still on the throne, however blatantly and confidently the little lords of earth may exercise their dominion.

The Lord's Prayer is not only a prayer to "repeat" until it loses its meaning by "dull repetition." It is a pattern for all our praying. And this is always the place to begin when we pray. Remember to whom we address ourselves—"Our Father who art in heaven." You are not coming to a friend to ask for a five-dollar loan. You are not coming to an excusing officer to get an excuse for something that you haven't done. You are not petitioning for a favor of one kind or another.

You are entering into the presence of "the Majesty on high."
You seek audience with the King!

And we dare to seek it, because we know that He is a loving Father, more ready to hear than we to pray, who wills for us only that which is for our good. For we have seen "the light of the knowledge of the glory of God in the face of Jesus Christ."

HALLOWED BE THY NAME

TEXT: *John 5:36-44*

THE SECOND PETITION, "Hallowed be thy name," must be considered in relation to the Second Commandment, "Thou shalt not take the name of the Lord thy God in vain." What is there stated negatively, is here stated positively. The Christian who prays as his Lord taught him earnestly seeks the Father's help in keeping the Second Commandment. It must be immediately apparent that no one really prays the Lord's Prayer, and then goes out to use the Holy Name lightly or loosely.

But it can surely be questioned whether we exhaust the content of this petition by this negative reference. We are asking for more than assistance against the temptation to profanity. We are not assuming a position of neutrality over against the divine Name; we are asking that we lend ourselves to His purposes in such a way that it will reflect credit upon our Father who is in heaven.

In the passage which we have read, Jesus claims to have come in His Father's name. The works which He was doing in their midst "bear me witness that the Father has sent me." It was because they did not believe Him that they could not receive "the glory that comes from the only God." Elsewhere He said, "He who has seen me has seen the Father." Therefore, what we do to Christ is what we do to God. To accept the witness of the Father which comes to us through Christ is the clear obligation of those who pray this petition. Thus we honor the Father. To reject Him whom He has sent is to reject the Father who sent Him.

So we understand this petition properly only when we respond in faith to Christ. Unless we trust God and commit our own lives to Him in faith, nothing that we can do with our lives will "hallow" His name. Neither words nor deeds, however laudatory they may be, can ever substitute for that deep inner surrender of our inmost beings to the Father whom we have come to know in Jesus Christ.

But with this starting point, we can speak of a life that honors God. Jesus says that His followers are "the light of the world." They are like "a city set on a hill" which cannot be hid. "Let your light so shine before men, that they may see your good works and give glory to your Father who is in heaven." Here is really the nub of the Christian life. It is not too terribly difficult to be good in such a way that we stand out conspicuously and draw attention to ourselves. There are ostentatious ways of being good, and not all of them are expensive. But to do good in such a way that we fade out of the picture and men look past us to God, this is not easy. It is better to have men say, "What a great God he has" than it is to have them say, "What a good man he is."

I say, it is not easy thus to glorify God by our good works. And it cannot be taught in the sense that some prescription can be given for it. In its very nature this kind of service is spontaneous, uncalculating, "does not insist on its own way." It is the reflection of one's own nature, and does not need to be coerced by the consideration of probable rewards. But I would make two observations that may be relevant, if we want to be the kind of persons whose works will lead men "to glorify your Father who is in heaven." The first is this: Make no secret of your dependence upon Him. Let men know that He is the source of your life and faith and hope. Of course, there is a conspicuous way of doing this, too, which attracts attention to ourselves. But it can be done in humble and inconspicuous ways, that leave no doubt of the sincerity of your profession. The second observation is this: We are more likely to reflect honor upon God in our good works if we are in the habit of doing good.

There is a notion abroad that we are more likely to be ethical when we break the pattern of habit, when we consciously and perhaps agonizingly make a decision. Of course, it is sometimes true that doing the right calls for a clear and difficult choice. Habit may often be on the side of selfish concerns. But this need not be the case. It is part of our Christian assignment to develop characteristic ways of acting that will become habitual in the good sense. We can cultivate generous attitudes by reacting generously to situations that confront us. In the measure that we do, the good which we accomplish seems less of an accomplishment to us. In the end we may be able to say, even when we have done all that is commanded, "We are unworthy servants; we have only done what was our duty." That kind of attitude, which claims no credit for itself, will reflect credit upon the God we serve.

It would, of course, be a gross error to assume that by any action of ours we could confer upon God some honor or glory which was not already His. As Luther reminds us, "God's name is indeed holy of itself." We can only acknowledge His holiness by rendering Him the obedience, faith, and love which are His due. But among us, in our individual lives or in our lives together, it is by no means evident that God receives the honor which is due His name. Would we dare to say about our life as a college family that the overwhelming impression which an observer would have is that this is a place where the highest honor is shown to God? Or would he be more impressed by our failure in this regard than by our achievement? And as a nation, which frequently asserts its

Christian ideals over against the loud and blatant godlessness of some other parts of the world, can we really claim that God always occupies the highest place in our loyalty and devotion.

We are indeed a "churchgoing" people beyond that of most parts of the world. A visitor from almost any country who remains over Sunday cannot but be impressed by the relatively larger portions of our population who attend services compared to the country from which he comes. It is probable, too, that we are building more churches proportionately than are the Christians of most other lands. We are not likely to underestimate the significance of these places of worship. The new chapel soon to be erected on this campus will mean much to us, and we may assume that churches mean as much in all the communities of our country.

But even as we speak of our advantage in the matter of our worship, we tend to draw attention to ourselves and our own virtues. It is not thus that we honor God's name. Ought we not rather wonder how it can be, with all our worshiping multitudes and with all our places of worship, that there are so many marks of growing moral and spiritual decay in our midst? If we seek the answer to that question in our worship, with humble and penitent hearts, we will truly honor God.

THY KINGDOM COME

TEXT: *Matthew 9:35; 12:28; 13:24-30*

IT WOULD BE A WHOLESOME EXPERIENCE for any preacher on this subject first to ascertain what his listeners have been praying for when they have prayed, "Thy kingdom come." There is surely no prayer which you have uttered more frequently than the Lord's Prayer, including this petition that His kingdom come. I wonder what has been in your mind as you have voiced this request again and again.

For one thing, the very idea of a "kingdom" is foreign to us. A republic perhaps, or a democracy, we could understand. Kingship has largely been a casualty of progress, at least in the Western world. Those who remain in the position of kings have either become nominal and representative figures, or are relics of a bygone era. But it may well be argued that "kingdom" is the right word here. If it has a failing, it is not that it claims too much for the sovereign, but that all kingship as we know it is qualified in one way or another. It is qualified, for instance, by the limitations of the sovereign.

Few monarchs have been able to stand as much power and authority as they have gathered to themselves. Lord Acton's dictum that "power corrupts and absolute power corrupts absolutely" finds its richest documentation, though not its only one, in the records of royalties. The imperfections of kings has attached itself to the kingdoms over which they have presided, so that when one speaks of the "kingdom of God" one must be careful not to import these human imperfections and even perversions into it. The earthly kingships are qualified also by the character of the allegiance which can be claimed from subjects. The power of the earthly king has its visible evidence in the means for coercing unwilling subjects. This is at once the evidence of sovereign power and of the failure to command the complete loyalty and obedience of the subjects. One who would be completely sovereign would not need to coerce obedience. It is, therefore, somewhat questionable whether one should introduce the idea of coercive power into the conception of the kingdom of God.

With this caution, let us see whether we can briefly give content to the kingdom for whose coming we have so often prayed. The basic element in it is usually identified as "the rule of God," or the "realm of God." Perhaps one can say that it is a relationship more than a place, but since the relationship involves people, a community, it is not adequate to think of it apart from some location in which the community exists. Although it is quite distinctly a New Testament concept, it has its clear counterpart in the Old Testament; the covenant people, the people of God, and the faithful remnant. They stood in a special relationship of blessing and obedience to the God who called Abraham, Isaac, and Jacob; who led them out of bondage in Egypt, and turned them into a nation. They were to be a dedicated community. When they failed as a nation, the faithful remnant became the vehicle by which God accomplished His purpose.

But the kingdom comes in quite a different way when Christ comes to the world. In Him God rules completely, for He is wholly subject to the Father's will. "I seek not my own will but the will of him who sent me." He is the only complete instance of "the rule of God" which history offers. However, Christ is not only the one instance of the completely willing subject of God's rule; He is also the God who rules. He is the incarnate Son of God. The grace and power of God are present in Him and through Him. "If it is by the Spirit of God that I cast out demons, then the kingdom of God has come upon you."

When Jesus began His preaching in Galilee, according to Mark, He did so with the announcement, "The time is fulfilled, and the kingdom of God is at hand; repent, and believe in the gospel." Some New Testament scholars argue that the proper translation here is "the kingdom of God has come." At least, there can be no doubt that Jesus asserted that the kingdom of God was present with Him and was being offered through Him to all men. Many of the parables of the kingdom, especially the parables of growth, describe a reality which is already present. It is present in the sense that the possibility of fellowship with God through Jesus Christ is present. It becomes actual in the measure that men respond in faith and love to His gospel. Thus the idea of the kingdom comes to incorporate the responding community. Both Jesus and His disciples belong in the kingdom of God.

But with a marked difference! In the disciples the rule of God is a frail and flickering thing. They hardly know whether they dare to believe in Him. They stand confused and uncertain before His announcement that He must go to Jerusalem to suffer and to die. They are shattered by the events of Holy Week—the betrayal, the arrest, the denial, the crucifixion. "We had hoped that he was the one to redeem Israel," they said on Easter afternoon. It was only gradually, after His appearances, and His ascension, and then the day of Pentecost, that they came to understand how He had triumphed through it all, and how their fellowship with God through Christ had been fixed forever by His dying and rising again. As they came to understand the meaning of it, they could speak of "the kingdom of God" with greater confidence and clarity. And at the center of their thought of the kingdom was the Christ in whom they believed and to whom they had committed themselves. It was, indeed, "the kingdom of his beloved Son, in whom we have redemption, the forgiveness of sins." Over against those who made of it something too external and visible, they asserted that "the kingdom of God does not mean food and drink but righteousness and peace and joy in the Holy Spirit." But equally, against those who were tempted to claim the spiritual inheritance without visible amendment of life, they asserted that "no immoral or impure man, or one who is covetous (that is, an idolater) has any inheritance in the kingdom of Christ and of God." And apparently there were those who thought pious words could be substituted for righteous lives; Paul warns them that "the kingdom of God does not consist in talk but in power."

They knew themselves to be members of the kingdom of Christ and of God here and now, but they knew also that what they now had was but a foretaste, a down payment, of what was coming. The rule of God which was perfect and complete in Christ was imperfect and incomplete in them. What they had was a guarantee of what would come when Christ had completely established His dominion. And this could not happen until they had come to share fully in His death and resurrection, by their own dying and rising again, unless indeed He were to return in triumph to claim His own first. But there could be no doubt about the outcome any more. His death and resurrection had taken away the sting of death.

What then do we pray for in this petition? If we pray it aright, we pray that God may have His way with us; that we may respond to His gospel in faith and obedience; that we may know the fellowship with God through Jesus Christ here and now; that we may be firmly anchored in the sure hope of an eternal life beyond all of our tomorrows. It is not a little thing for which we pray!

THY WILL BE DONE, ON EARTH
AS IT IS IN HEAVEN

TEXT: *Hebrews 13:20-21*

ONE OF THE PERENNIAL HAZARDS for the Christian is to accept the comforts of his religion, and neglect its responsibilities. Jesus seems to have anticipated that this would be the case. As though He feared that men would interpret the "kingdom" with too little concern for the needs of this world and time, He proceeds immediately to specify the meaning of the kingdom in terms of obedience to His will here and now. "Thy will be done, on earth as it is in heaven."

The real point in this petition is not that we should know for sure and agree upon what specific things God wills for us in our complex modern world; the point is that God's will is never approved or accepted or embraced by us except by doing it now. That is, one cannot accept the will of God "in principle." One can only accept God's will by acting upon it in some specific and concrete sense and in the situation in which one now stands. Even God's will to forgive must be accepted anew each day in each new circumstance. The "old Adam" must be "drowned and destroyed by daily sorrow and repentance," and "the new man should daily come forth and rise," was the way Luther expressed it.

It would be so much more comfortable if the "will of God"

were the sort of thing which one could discuss in a detached way, as an abstraction. It would be such an excellent subject for a high level "session" in a dormitory room or around a campfire. One could discuss "the will of God" as one discusses Plato's "world of ideas" or Rousseau's "general will." There would be enlightenment in such a discussion, a laying bare of minds, and perhaps even a fair amount of emotion generated. I do not speak altogether without experience here. Perhaps you have been in on some such discussion, too. I guess one's mind can be less profitably employed than in "discussing" God. But the danger is that we shall think that God's will has somehow been done when it has been talked about; we assume that having an accurate opinion of what God wants done in the world is the same as doing what God wants done.

The only adequate response to God's will is a decision to act. This implies that action which flows from it, for a decision which is not acted upon is a decision not to act. We cannot substitute an inquiry in the realm of knowledge for a decision in the realm of obedience. There is that disturbing statement of Jesus always to reckon with: "My teaching is not mine, but his who sent me; if any man's will is to do his will, he shall know whether the teaching is from God or whether I am speaking on my own authority." Whereas in many fields we must know in order to act, in matters of faith we must be willing to act in order to know.

All of this Jesus implied when He taught His disciples to pray, "Thy will be done on earth." Each time we pray His prayer we commit ourselves to action here and now. For the Christian, the total basis of action in every sphere of his activity must be related to this petition. It is not as though one were adding another basis of judgment to those which he already has; one is substituting this basis for all others. One is committing himself to put his whole life into the context of God's will.

137

A difficulty for many people is the tendency to see God's will and prompting only in the unusual situation and the exceptional experience. The God who made us creatures with physical needs, wills that those needs shall be met, and we may properly feel that we are doing His will when we do what is necessary in order to meet them, unless we violate other commandments in the way we meet them. God wills that we shall develop the potentialities for service which He has given us, and we may properly feel about the whole enterprise in which we are engaged in preparation for lives of service that this is within the context of His will. The choice of vocation is a point at which the will of God for us usually becomes relevant and often disturbing. We are likely to seek some special evidence of God's "call," especially if one of the alternatives involves religious service.

I would not want to deny the possibility of such "inner" guidance, some supplemental direction, at this point where we are making a choice that will affect our total life service in such a profound and extensive fashion. But it is well for us to remember that if God has a plan for our lives, He didn't just think it up when we begin to get concerned about it. He had it when He gave us the talents and resources with which we have been endowed. We do well to consult our endowments when we seek to know His will. And His unseen but powerful hand may well have been guiding us along the way, even when we knew it not. It may be well to consult our experiences in the past, to see the direction of our lives and interests. All of this is not to say that there are not decisive and even dramatic turns in the road for some of us, and His will may be in them, but it is not necessary that there should be such decisive and dramatic events in order that we may be assured of our calling.

It is a sure rule that if a person would know more of God's will for him than he now knows, he must do as much of it as he knows. Often we cannot see the way ahead, until we have moved farther down the road.

But what shall we say about the doing of God's will in the larger patterns and structures of society? God's will for the world is not exhausted by His will for individuals. For instance, it is clear that God does not will wars, or those conditions that make for war. He wills justice and, therefore, those conditions that make for justice. He does not will disease or poverty, and therefore He is concerned that the conditions which cause them should be abolished.

It is not enough to think of this aspect of the divine Will solely in terms of individual generous action. The amount of generous action in which one can engage and the measure of responsible freedom which one can exercise is not the same under fascist or communist forms of government as it is in a democracy. The forms of political or social structure under which one lives affects the good that can be done in the world. And, equally, it must be insisted, the failures of democracy to be true to itself must be of concern to anyone who prays that God's will may be done on earth. If justice and freedom are denied to any of a nation's citizens, the Christian must be disturbed, and actively seek to correct that failure.

It is not really as difficult as we sometimes think to agree on what kind of world God's will would bring into being, if it were obeyed. The biggest difficulty arises in the way that it is to be achieved. Here we can afford differences, for none of us knows the way too well. We need to be confronted by alternate ways; we can all learn from one another. But the basic commandment which is laid upon all men, individually and collectively, is that they shall act out of love toward others. And love is not a sentiment which we may indulge; it is actual concern for our neighbor's welfare. We must use all our resources of intelligence and character, all the means provided by our callings, to do good to all men.

139

GIVE US THIS DAY OUR DAILY BREAD

TEXT: *Luke 4:16-21; 1 John 3:17*

THE THREE PETITIONS which have already been considered provide the frame within which all prayer must be placed. The prime objective of the Christian in all his praying is that God shall have His way. That we shall secure our wishes is at best a secondary consideration, and subject always to the condition that what we ask for is consistent with the hallowing of God's name, the furtherance of His will, and the coming of His kingdom.

We may properly derive some encouragement from the fact that Jesus started where we are most inclined to start; He started with our physical needs. As the passage from Luke's Gospel indicates, Jesus' concern for men's physical needs was no mere afterthought, a sort of concession to the weakness of men. He found the key text for His own ministry in a passage out of the prophet Isaiah which speaks of "good news to the poor," "release to the captives," "recovering of sight to the blind," and "liberty for the oppressed."

If one compares Jesus with other religious teachers, with whom He is sometimes compared, one is impressed by a kind of "earthiness" and realism in His views. Our actual physical needs are so obvious that it should be perfectly apparent to us that God wants to provide for them. Does He not even care for the birds of the air and the flowers of the field? "Your heavenly Father knows that you need them all." There is no reason for anxiety about these things.

But there is reason for praying for them, nonetheless; otherwise we would not have this petition included in the Lord's Prayer. And there can be no doubt that there have been times when this petition has been prayed with real earnestness. Indeed, there are many people in many lands for whom this is probably the most conscious and continuous prayer which is ever uttered. Hunger and famine are perennial companions of the human race, and the majority of mankind probably still go to bed each night with their physical hunger unsatisfied.

But we are likely not among them. To be sure, there are students who have financial problems; even some who do not eat as they should here at Gustavus. And still, hunger is hardly a problem here on our campus. Although the generalization would have to provide for some exceptions, hunger is hardly a problem anywhere in our country. We are far more conscious of the problem of surpluses than we are of the problem of scarcity. At least it is a fair prediction that those of you who are within the hearing of my voice will not lack bread for the day. We may lack things that we want or even that we need; we may sometimes eat hamburger when we would prefer steak; but hunger in the sense that vast sections of the world understand the term is not apt to be an actual experience for us.

The question then is this: How does one pray sincerely for daily bread when tables are well filled and storehouses loaded with food? In the first place, we should be reminded by this petition that our daily bread is a gift of God. Food is still grown; it is not manufactured. There is plenty of manufacture in the processing of it, but no one has succeeded in producing a synthetic food which could dispense with natural growth, at least none that people can be induced to eat. I would be less confident about that assertion, if I had not heard it from the world-famous biochemist, Anton J. Carlson of the University of Chicago, when he visited Gustavus a few years ago. This means that the decisive factors of sunshine and rain, and to some extent fertility, are beyond the control of man. They are gifts of the Creator through the natural process of life and growth and death. And in a society in which we must work in order to acquire the fruits of nature, the capacity to work, with all the physical and mental endowments which this implies, must be considered to be related to this petition.

While we are called upon to develop our potentialities, we must not overlook the potentialities themselves. These, surely, are God-given. When we pray this petition, we may properly include the care of our bodies, the development of our skills, the improvement of our minds, and the whole range of our knowledge by which we will be able to take our places as productive members of society, both within the home and within the economic structure by which daily bread is provided for our society. In all of this, surely, we have every right as Christians to enlist the aid of our heavenly Father and we are under obligation to recognize the extent to which we are dependent upon His gifts to us.

Secondly, we ought to place particular emphasis on the plural pronoun when our own tables are well filled. "Give us this day our daily bread." An unmarried friend of mine told me once that he had changed the pronoun to singular in the petitions of the Lord's Prayer, since this seemed to make it more personal, and then one day he realized that he had really changed the prayer. He was not praying as Jesus had taught when he prayed only for "my daily bread." The plural pronoun had to be there. Why would the Lord be more interested in the state of our table than He is in the state of every man's table? Here the second passage of Scripture speaks to the point: "But if any one has the world's goods and sees his brother in need, yet closes his heart against him, how does God's love abide in him?"

You remember the parable of the rich man and Lazarus, the beggar who was brought each day to his gate to eat the crumbs which had fallen from the rich man's table. There was something about that sort of callous indifference to another's physical need which touched Jesus to the quick. It is the very antithesis of the Christian spirit. The Christian cannot stand to see another suffer, if he has the means to alleviate his suffering. This is not to say that there are no Christians who do not respond in this way, but most of those who do not have some sense of unworthiness or inconsistency in connection with their failure, and must offer some rationalization for their conduct.

As Americans we can take some pride in the way our fathers responded to the problem of scarcity. They came to a new land, conquered the trackless wilderness and converted it into fields and factories. It has been claimed, and impressively supported, that their religious outlook had something to do with the initiative and drive which carried this land to almost unimagined heights of productivity. The problem now is not the problem of scarcity; it is the problem of abundance.

A crucial question, for which the answer has not yet been given, is whether we have the character and the religious outlook which will convert our abundance into blessing for the world. In part it is a question of disposition—do we have a mind to help others? In part it is a very complicated question of how to do it. To dump surpluses abroad poses serious problems. To use the vehicle of government for such assistance seems to do something to the spirit of generosity in the giver, and does not always bring gratitude or even friendliness from the recipient. Private philanthropy has its limitations, too, even if it be the philanthropy of Christian men and organizations.

It is not easy for us in this land of plenty to pray aright, "Give us this day our daily bread."

FORGIVE US OUR TRESPASSES, AS WE FORGIVE THOSE WHO TRESPASS AGAINST US

TEXT: *Matthew 18:21-35*

HERE IS THAT SAME COMPLICATING PLURAL PRONOUN AGAIN: "Forgive us our trespasses." One might think that it would be enough to pray for personal forgiveness. Repentance and the sense of guilt are very personal matters; how can we presume to speak for others in the matter of forgiveness?

There is at least one implication that is immediately apparent. If we use the plural pronoun without qualification, we must include those who have offended against us. By what authorization would we exclude those whom we have not forgiven? Perhaps this is the key to the second part of the petition. Many New Testament scholars have puzzled about it, and perhaps most of us have wondered about the adequacy of divine forgiveness that is patterned after the forgiveness which we extend to those who trespass against us.

It is complicated also by the fact that we do not have unanimity among the writers of the Gospels as to precisely how Jesus phrased this petition. Matthew and Luke record the Lord's Prayer, but neither of them gives precisely the form with which we are most familiar. Matthew substitutes "debts" for

144

"trespasses"; Luke has "sins," and then introduces a somewhat different thought—"for we ourselves also forgive everyone that is indebted to us." If we are uneasy about Matthew's version in which we pray for forgiveness in the measure in which we have forgiven, we must certainly flinch at this claim that we always forgive everyone who is indebted to us. The facts do not seem to accord with the statement. It is not that easy to forgive.

It is, of course, quite possible that Jesus used this pattern prayer on more than one occasion, and that He did not use exactly the same wording each time. We shall not enter into the literary problem here. Whichever version we choose, there is still a problem for the pray-er in this petition. How can we honestly pray for forgiveness "as we forgive those who trespass against us"? If we were fashioning our own petition, surely we would pray for a more clear, unequivocal forgiveness than that. Perhaps the clue lies in the plural pronoun. The prayer for forgiveness is a prayer that all men may be forgiven, including those who have trespassed against us. It is a prayer to a gracious God, and God is the God of all men. This most intimate and personal need is also the need of all men. If we have any concern for others at all, we must include them in this petition. If we have no concern for others, there is no possibility of forgiveness. Such complete self-centeredness is only seeking to use God, not to serve Him.

There are two seemingly contradictory elements in the experience of the penitent sinner before God. One is that he must not shift the responsibility for his action from his own shoulders to another. "Father, I have sinned against heaven and before you; I am no longer worthy to be called your son," says the returning prodigal son. He does not blame his companions or his employers or the various circumstances which led to his downfall. Perhaps he might have found some excuse in the attitude of the elder brother. But genuine penitence does not seek excuses. It bears its own blame and assumes its own responsibility.

On the other hand, a genuinely penitent sinner knows that the influence of his own life has spilled over into the lives of others, and that he must accept some responsibility also for the failure of others. As parents, for instance, we have helped shape the moral standards of our children, and cannot wholly escape responsibility for their failures. As members of a student body, we have something to do with setting the "tone" or the "atmosphere" of a campus. When it is not what it ought to be, and others are led into unworthy courses of action, we cannot shrug our shoulders and say we have nothing to do with this. Cain's question, "Am I my brother's keeper"? was unworthy of him, and it is unworthy of us.

The rapidly mounting problem of juvenile delinquency is surely not exclusively a "juvenile problem." The power of adult example, the false values fostered by generations that have placed too much emphasis on material things, the all but universal willingness to get something for nothing, and behind it all the self-centeredness which we have tried so hard in our generation to justify and dignify, even while holding to the forms of religious observance—surely these have made their contributions to the tangled web in which so many of today's youth find themselves ensnared.

In the problem of divorce, so greatly aggravated by hasty "war marriages," are they alone responsible who have become the victims, or is there not a wider responsibility that affects us all? Who is to blame for war? And who could list all the contributors to the moral breakdown in the realm of sex? Are the crimes of violence committed under the influence of alcohol solely the responsibility of those who commit them? What about those who profit from their intoxication (and all of us do at least to the extent of getting presumed tax relief from liquor taxation), those who contribute to their unwholesome environments, or are content that things shall be as they are? There is reason for the plural pronoun, is there not? "Forgive us our trespasses."

And now we must return to the second part of this petition. Forgiveness is too real a need in our world for us to suppose that we can be part of the world's healing, and hold out islands of resentment toward those who have offended against us. They but share in our guilt. And our share in the world's guilt is much too great ever to think that we can live without the forgiving spirit. Without it, we cannot accept forgiveness. God does not rule by fiat or coercion, so that if He decides to forgive us we are forgiven regardless of whether we accept it or not. Forgiveness is not something that the postman can bring you, like a receipt for a bill that has been paid.

Forgiveness is a radical and shattering experience; at least, sometimes it is. It is like major surgery. It can be almost like dying. Indeed, the New Testament often speaks of the encounter with God through which we are forgiven and redeemed as dying and rising again. It is the surrender of ourselves to God. Paul says, "I have been crucified with Christ; it is no longer I who live, but Christ who lives in me; and the life I now live in the flesh I live by faith in the Son of God, who loved me and gave himself for me." "If any one is in Christ, he is a new creation." The center of his life has changed. Instead of being self-centered, self-reliant, self-justifying, he has come to rely on God's grace in Christ, and has become the agent of God's love. How can he deal with others less graciously than God has dealt with him?

If there is in you any remnant of an unforgiving spirit, this must be ranked high among the trespasses for which you seek forgiveness. And that prayer cannot be sincere unless you are willing to yield up every grudge and peeve by which your spiritual life is being throttled.

LEAD US NOT INTO TEMPTATION;
BUT DELIVER US FROM EVIL

TEXT: *1 Corinthians 10:12-13; James 1:12-15*

IT IS STRANGE how these familiar petitions of the Lord's Prayer, which we are able to "recite" so easily and so glibly, lead us into some of the most profound and difficult problems when one stops to look at them for a moment. The whole problem of evil is involved in this one, and any one who has wrestled with it even superficially knows that one does not dispose of evil with a sentence, or a paragraph, or a volume.

On the face of it, this petition seems to raise more questions regarding the problem of evil than it answers. For instance, it seems to imply that it is God who leads us into temptation, and that He must be solicited not to do so. And this surely plays into the hands of those who would blame God for the evils which infest our world. Of course, a more careful reading of Scripture would provide evidence of another source of temptation. James says clearly, "Let no one say when he is tempted, 'I am tempted of God.'" Paul speaks of Satan as the tempter. Jesus was tempted of Satan in the wilderness. One could amplify the Biblical references, if it were necessary.

It may be, therefore, that we should understand this petition as a prayer to be spared temptation; that we should be kept out of all circumstances in which we are likely to be tempted. But are we sure that we really want this? I have a feeling that life would be both dull and barren, if there were no temptation in it. It would be a life without moral choices, with no live alternatives that really matter. Some element of temptation is inherent in every decision that we make. Every circumstance in which we can find ourselves has some risk in it. Health and learning and prosperity hold temptations for us, as well as illness, ignorance, and poverty. To have a world in which all temptation has been removed would be to have a world without free agents confronted by moral choice—that is, a world without persons.

This is not to say that temptation is a good thing in itself; it is simply to recognize that it is a fact in all human existence, and that we shall have to live with it. In what sense ought we, then, to pray that we should not be led into temptation? In the sense, surely, that in the face of temptation we may be delivered from evil; that when faced by moral choices, we may be given the wisdom and the courage to choose the right and resist the wrong. We pray that we may not be overcome either by the evil that is without or the evil inclinations that are within.

There are at least two ways in which it seems to me this petition can be understood in addition to the simple prayer for strength to resist temptation in the ordinary sense of that word. The first is that we pray that we may not be led into circumstances where we do not know what is right and what is wrong; that we may be spared the agony of having to choose in the dark. I think a doctor must sometimes know this torture of having to choose a course of action with reference to a sick person, with insufficient knowledge of the nature of the ailment and of the proper prescription for the cure. There have been some rather significant novels written on that theme. A statesman must sometimes feel it as he faces the terribly complex and complicated political scene; a wrong decision may have disastrous consequences. It is not cowardice to pray that one may be spared this kind of decision. Any one's life can become so complicated, perhaps by his own wrong choices, that it is almost impossible to see any right choice open to him. Or a person may come into circumstances in which the pressures upon him to yield to his poorer nature and his baser self seem to be greater than he can bear. It is not cowardly or improper to pray that one should be spared those circumstances. We may well be grateful as students and teachers, for instance, that we are not subjected to the pressures to which students and teachers in some parts of the world are being subjected to embrace godless atheism in order to qualify for scholarships and promotions. We may well pray that we may be spared this "temptation."

The second concrete sense in which we may understand this petition has reference to trials and persecutions. In both the passages to which we have referred, this is plainly included. In First Corinthians, Paul refers to temptations that are to be borne, and encourages the readers to believe that "God will not let you be tempted beyond your strength, but with the temptation will also provide the way of escape." James speaks of the man "who endures trial" and promises that "when he has stood the test he will receive the crown of life which God has promised to those who love him." This may seem rather irrelevant to us, who are not likely to suffer persecution of any serious sort for our faith, but we cannot be so insulated from what is going on in the world around us as not to know that it is as relevant to many of our fellow Christians as it was in the days of Paul and of James. This kind of temptation does not stem from our disobedience to God's will but from faithfulness to it. When temptation is understood in this sense, the petition "Lead us not into temptation" seems properly addressed to God, for it is God's leading then which brings the trial upon His followers, even though their suffering is inflicted by evil men.

However we are to understand the first part of this double petition, the second part seems clear, and it must be allowed to throw light on the first. We pray to be delivered from "evil" or from "the evil one." The Christian is not spared the encounter with evil, above his fellows. But he has a source of strength, if he will use it, which is more than equal to the foe. And because so much of the evil which is against us is in our own hearts and minds—in our self-interest and self-confidence—there is real healing and help for us in acknowledging our need of deliverance. When we pray, "Deliver us from evil," we are turning away from our self-centeredness and placing our reliance on God. In this turning to God there is real strength to resist temptation.

One final thought! We have spoken of temptation as though it were something which confronted us whether or not we desired it. Most of us will recognize that we often place ourselves voluntarily in circumstances which make it difficult for us to resist temptation. One might even say that we court it, as though it were something pleasant and exciting. Ernest Fremont Tittle makes a relevant observation at this point. He says, "With the help of God a man may be strong enough to resist temptation when it comes; but no man is strong enough to invite it."[5] We do not pray this petition sincerely if we invite temptation. We cannot expect God to be working for us, on our side, if we are working for the "evil one."

---

[5] *The Lord's Prayer*, Abingdon-Cokesbury, 1942, p. 113.

FOR THINE IS THE KINGDOM, AND THE POWER, AND THE GLORY, FOR EVER AND EVER

TEXT: *1 Timothy 1:12-17*

IN ONE SENSE, this is not a part of the Lord's Prayer. It does not appear in either of the versions which we have in the Gospels. It has been added by the disciples of the Lord, apparently from very early times, and has now become fixed in our minds as an appropriate conclusion to the petitions which we have considered. We may think of this concluding doxology as a contribution which the church through the ages has made to the Lord's Prayer. It constitutes a sort of endorsement by Christian generations throughout the church, by which we may be encouraged to believe that God can and will hear our prayers.

It is not a petition; it is a confession. It may, therefore, seem more properly to belong in the Creed than in the Lord's Prayer. We have already prayed for the "kingdom, and the power, and the glory." We have prayed, "Thy kingdom come," "Thy will be done," "Hallowed be thy name." We have solicited His power and goodness in asking for daily bread, the forgiveness of sins, and the power to resist temptation and to overcome evil. Here we only remind ourselves, as the church has through the ages reminded itself, that the kingdom and the power and the glory are already His. Therefore, we can believe that what we have prayed for will come to pass. He will hear us and answer us.

Perhaps we need this constant reminder that prayer is a confession of faith. "And whatever you ask in prayer, you will receive, if you have faith." Prayer is not a bargain counter at which we may exchange our little deeds of righteousness for great gifts from God. Prayer is not the result of cold calculation from which we have drawn the conclusion that we have more to gain than to lose by joining the ranks of the petitioners. Prayer is responding to God's overwhelming grace and power with the surrender of our whole beings; the acknowledgment that we have met our Sovereign and that henceforth we must take our direction from Him and rely on His power, which is at work within us "both to will and to work for his good pleasure." To be known among our fellows as one who prays to "Our Father who art in heaven," is to be known as one who believes that "Thine is the kingdom, and the power, and the glory, for ever and ever."

But dare we really make this kind of sweeping confession? Or, do we qualify this final confession in ways that weaken our prayers? I expect that many of us do. We do not really expect much from prayer, because we cannot really believe that the "kingdom and the power and the glory" are His alone. There are so many other powers at work in the world which are more visible and more demanding. There are "dominions" which seem to have much more to do with our daily bread, for instance, than "the kingdom of God." The economic system and the economic cycle, prosperity and depression, getting the right job and knowing the right people—these obviously influence what we can afford to put on the table. Decisions made in Washington or London or Berlin or Moscow have evident bearing on the freedom which we may enjoy to carry out our plans for our lives, economically and in every other respect.

A "call to arms" from our earthly government can take us from our jobs and our families and shatter our plans for our future. Do we dare to believe that over and above all of these things there is a kingdom and power and glory which is God's alone?

It must be frankly acknowledged that this is a declaration of faith; it is not something that can be proved by any sort of survey of all the facts. This is not a conclusion which could be so effectively argued that every rational person would have to accept it. The Christian has come to this conclusion because he has learned about Jesus Christ. Especially, because he has learned about Christ's death and resurrection. God revealed himself to be the final Sovereign of life and the world when He raised Jesus from the dead; and when He established a kingdom on this earth against which "the powers of death" cannot prevail. We know ourselves to be part of "a kingdom that cannot be shaken." Therefore, we can believe all that the Scriptures tell us regarding "the mighty acts of God" and His final triumph.

But, looking out upon the world from this vantage point, we are not without supporting evidence. For one thing, the history of the church itself, its very survival among the hostile powers which have surrounded and often opposed it, is sort of a miracle. Of course, one must admit that the church has not always resisted the temptation to use the weapons of the world in its battle to survive, but it has been the strongest when it has been most true to its own spiritual weapons. If one reviews the list of the empires which have stood up in their pride and tried to destroy the church during these centuries, and are now part of the rubble and ruin of history, one cannot deny that the church seems to have "staying power" beyond that of most of the kingdoms of this world.

And then, if one thinks of the kingdom of God in the broader sense as including God's total rule of nature and history and conscience, there surely seem to be limits set upon the kind of divergence which God permits to survive. The completely "lawless" person isolates himself from society and destroys himself. God's universe will not indefinitely tolerate the total disregard of God's law. It is not only in a religious sense that "the wages of sin is death." Most ways of sinning are short cuts to dying. At least, it is not difficult to demonstrate that there is some connection between dissipation and the breakdown of health. There are, however, enough exceptions to the rule to forbid drawing conclusions from the state of one's health to the state of one's soul. What is true of the limits set upon the individual's freedom to disregard God and His laws without suffering the consequences is true also of societies and nations. It may be less evident than in the case of individuals, because group processes are usually slower than the life processes of individuals. A man may destroy himself through indulgence within a few years; for a nation it may take several generations.

And whose is "the glory"? That is the decisive question. If we claim the glory for ourselves, we cannot share in His kingdom or His power. In Paul's classic description of fallen man, recounted in the first chapter of his letter to the Romans, the central theme is this: ". . . for although they knew God they did not honor him as God or give thanks to him, but they became futile in their thinking and their senseless minds were darkened. Claiming to be wise, they became fools, and exchanged the glory of the immortal God for images resembling mortal man or birds or animals or reptiles." From this failure to honor God flows every form of corruption and decay.

It may be that we in America are in danger of forgetting to whom the glory belongs. We claim so much and are so confident that what we do is the right and that what we achieve is the best. It is true of nations and of individuals that "pride goes before a fall." Self-glorification is the beginning of the disintegration of national strength and character.

AMEN

TEXT: *2 Corinthians 1:19-22*

THERE IS NO DOUBT that "Amen" is a popular word in the religious vocabulary of many people, especially of those who tolerate religion rather than practice it. This popularity is almost certainly based on a total misunderstanding of its meaning. It is assumed that it announces the termination of a prayer or a sermon, which of course is true. But it terminates a prayer the way a signature terminates a check, or a mortgage, or a wedding license. One ought not to be reckless about the use of it, for it carries implications.

We have suggested that the doxology, "For thine is the kingdom, and the power, and the glory," may be thought of as the contribution which the church has made to the Lord's Prayer through the centuries. In using it, we add our voices to the voices of countless Christians who have thus testified to their faith in the Father to whom our prayer is addressed. But this final word, "Amen," is our own personal contribution and endorsement. It is our "signature." By its use we claim the whole of the Lord's Prayer as our own. We affirm that what He has taught us to pray is really our own prayer.

There is a powerful and dramatic scene described in the Old Testament which may help us to understand the import of this word. Moses is preparing to turn over the leadership of the people of Israel, knowing that his own time with them will be

156

brief. He calls the people together before they pass over the Jordan into the Land of Promise, and instructs them how to proceed when they have crossed over. Addressing the assembled multitude, he says, "Keep silence, and hear, O Israel: This day you have become the people of the Lord your God. You shall therefore obey the voice of the Lord your God, keeping his commandments and his statutes, which I command you this day." This covenant relationship is to be certified and sealed when they cross the Jordan. The Levites are to read the laws, one by one, and after each one "all the people shall answer and say, 'Amen.'" This single word, "Amen," became the commitment on which a nation was founded and set aside as a "people of God."

In the last book of the Bible, the Revelation, one of the titles by which Christ is designated is "the Amen." In Second Corinthians, from which we have drawn our text, Paul says that "all the promises of God find their Yes in him." He confirms in His own person and by His dying and rising again every promise which has ever been given. The promise made to Abraham and to Isaac and Jacob, the promises made to Israel, the promises made to the faithful remnant, all are confirmed and validated in Christ. But more than that, every evidence of God's goodness—sun and rain and growing things, curious minds, the love of home and friends, the thrill of achievement—is confirmed by the triumph of God's love and power in Jesus Christ. God has said "Amen" to it all in accents which cannot be misunderstood.

But there is an Amen to be spoken also by us. Since all the promises of God find their Yes in Him, we must utter our "Amen, through him, to the glory of God." That is, by our faith in Christ and our surrender to Him, we also affirm the promises of God.

When we place the Amen of our lips at the end of this prayer, we are saying that we intend, honestly and earnestly, to put our lives behind its every petition. It is almost as though we made a vow, before God and our fellow men, to live as we have prayed. Therefore, the real test of sincerity with regard to this word, especially, is what we do after we have said it. It is not, as we sometimes suppose, the sign that we have finished the prayer; it is the commitment that it will stay with us as our guiding light. We will indeed look for the answer, but we will also work as we have prayed.

We are never through with praying, and Amen is the sign of it. It is the connecting link between our words and our deeds. Therefore, it is placed appropriately at the end of all our prayers. It has its place in the liturgies of the church as the congregation confirms the petitions offered in its behalf by the officiating pastor. Wherever it occurs, it involves this complete commitment.

Amen is a little word, but it takes a life—a dedicated life—to exhaust its meaning.

PARTS FOUR AND FIVE

The Sacraments
Holy Baptism
The Lord's Supper

BY GRACE ARE YOU SAVED

TEXT: *Ephesians 2:4-10*

"GRACE" IS A LOVELY WORD. It has been called the most beautiful word in the English language. It is a complimentary word, even when we use it superficially. To speak of someone's walk or bearing as "graceful" is to voice a compliment. To speak of a person as "gracious" is to extend the compliment to something inward and to make a favorable judgment about one's total personality.

But "grace" is really a religious word. One could write a good deal of the history of the Christian Church around the various meanings that the word has carried. There has been the assertion that grace is something which God gives to men, as a sort of energizing force or power, a semi-substantial character that is infused into the believer and enables him to live a better life, to do "good works." This "infused grace" has been understood to come to believers primarily through the sacraments. This is the characteristic position of the Roman Catholic Church and is a key conception in much Roman theology and practice. Since it is mediated through the sacraments, it can be taken away by being deprived of the sacraments. Since the priest determines the qualifications for receiving the sacraments, and can withhold them at his discretion, he quite literally and logically stands guard over the access of the believer to the grace of God.

Mediated grace

161

But there is another understanding of the word "grace" which is central and basic in the evangelical view of the gospel. Luther described his own restless and agonizing quest in terms of the question, "How can I find a gracious God"? He became convinced that the grace of God was not something that God gives to men, but the gracious will of God, the character of God himself. It is God's desire to forgive—His "forgivingness." It is God's nature to forgive. Nothing can stand in the way of it except our unwillingness to accept it. No one can withhold it; it does not depend on any "good work" done in advance or in co-operation with the "infused grace" which God gives the seeking sinner. It is offered freely to any and all who will receive it. "For by grace you have been saved through faith; and this is not your own doing, it is the gift of God."

But we do speak of "means of grace." And when we thus speak we are talking about the Word and the Sacraments of Baptism and the Lord's Supper. They are the means in which and through which God makes known His graciousness. They are given us in order that we might know that God forgives us.

This is not to deny that we may know something about God apart from these means. God has not left himself without a witness even among those who know not the gospel. Some knowledge of God's existence can be seen in the universal recognition that there is some power not our own at work in the world. Just because we are creatures who inevitably stand before forces which are not under our control, we are likely to recognize the existence of some power greater than ourselves, even if we label it Chance or Fate. We can learn something about God from nature and from history and from the workings of conscience within us. Immanuel Kant is not the only one who would have to confess that the "starry heavens above" and "the moral law within" fill him with wonder. One can

162

learn something about God from test tubes and rocks and the working of the human mind, but one cannot know a gracious God from any of these—at least not in the sense in which we are here speaking.

This comes only through the Word of God, written and spoken, and through the sacraments. For it is only here we are confronted by the God and Father of our Lord Jesus Christ. It is only here that we learn of a love that was willing to die for sinners. There is no other channel through which we can learn about the incarnate Son of God who came into this world and loved men even unto death. "God shows his love for us in that while we were yet sinners, Christ died for us." There is no other gospel of "the remission of sins" save that good news which Christ proclaimed and which He actualized in His own dying and rising again. "God so loved the world that he gave his only Son, that whoever believes in him should not perish but have eternal life." You will never find that written in the sunset or in green forests, or in test tubes or the farthest reaches of the human mind. We would not know it except for the Word of God as it confronts us in the pages of Scripture, the service of the church, and most especially in the sacraments.

So treasure these "means of grace," for without them you would not know a gracious God.

HOLY BAPTISM

TEXT: *Matthew 28:18, 19*
Baptizing them in the name of the Father, and of the Son, and of the Holy Ghost.

THERE ARE NO CHRISTIANS WHO DO NOT BAPTIZE. I believe that generalization holds today and that it has been true throughout Christian history. There have been differences of opinion and conviction as to the meaning of baptism, the method of baptism, and the appropriate age at which baptism should take place; but there is universal recognition among Christians that baptism has an important place in the witness of the church and in the life of the Christian.

It may be assumed that most of you, if not all, have been baptized. So you may properly be asked to think about its meaning. Surely you must not be permitted to assume that it was merely a public or semi-public event in which you were given a name which would always be yours, unless you chose legally to change it.

You were baptized into the "name of the Father, and of the Son, and of the Holy Ghost." This assumes that we are not by nature bearers of that Name. We belong to a fallen humanity which does not automatically and naturally acknowledge the sovereignty of God's name. However romantic we may want to be about childhood, none of us can very convincingly argue that self-will, self-centeredness, is not the char-

164

acteristic mark of all human existence. Growing up is in part a matter of harnessing that self-will and directing it into less destructive channels, or at least masking it so that it assumes more acceptable forms. Faith is the transcendence of that self-will; it is the surrender of ourselves to God, and the acceptance of His will in trustful obedience.

Baptism is the rite by which Christian parents and a Christian congregation bring this new life into the believing community. It is the means, the event, in which, according to Christ's institution and command, those who are outside the church are brought into it. In some sense this is true even among those branches of Christendom that await a conscious experience of faith and a definite commitment before administering baptism.

If we ask how this can be—how the simple act of baptism with water can change the status of a person in his relation to the Church and to God—we will have to answer that we do not know. We practice baptism in obedience to Christ's command; we believe that His command and promise are sure.

But if we ask what this means to us—that we have been baptized—then there are some things that we can say.

First, we can say that our baptism established the conditions under which we can claim membership in Christ's Church. We were brought as infants, in the arms of another, without any record of good works, with no credits to our account, and we were made members of His Church. It has been said that infant baptism is the purest preaching of the gospel. Here the gospel of God's free grace is acted out before the congregation, as a new life is made the recipient of all God's blessings and full participant in the fellowship which we have with God through Christ.

There may be times when we will need to remember that—times when it is hard for us to believe that we have done enough to merit His grace. There will be times when we are tempted to doubt our claim to membership in the body of Christ. Luther said he often drove the devil away with the reminder that he had been baptized. Some of his critics have understood this to mean that Luther thought that any one who had been baptized would surely be saved. Such a conclusion would certainly find difficulty accounting for Luther's own earnest, even desperate and agonizing search for peace with God. What Luther meant was that God had accepted him as an infant, without anything to his account, and therefore He could be relied on to accept him on those same grounds now. "By grace you have been saved."

A second thing it means is that we have been incorporated into the life of a Christian congregation. This community of believers, and most especially the parents and the godparents, has assumed a responsibility for surrounding the baptized child with Christian love and instruction. Baptism is not an end but a beginning. It places responsibilities upon both the baptized one and the Christian community into which he is baptized. The planting of the seed does not guarantee the harvest, irrespective of soil and sun and rain.

The third thing we can say about it is this: If as baptized ones we are to reject Christ and the church, we must do so as rebels and traitors. We must do battle against our King and country as those who are within it. No longer do we have the choice of whether we are to be inside or outside. It is not one of the alternatives which we make now; it has already been made. If this seems slightly unfair, may I remind you that it is exactly the case with almost every meaningful relationship in life. You cannot reject your parents except as members of their family. You do not have the choice of the family into which you have come. You cannot reject America, except by insurrection and treachery, even though you were born here, and had nothing to say about whether you were to become American citizens. If you would oppose and seek to destroy America, you must do so as those who are already her citizens. And if you set yourselves against Christ and His Church—and there is no middle ground, "He who is not with me is against me"—you must do so as those who have already been made a part of her life.

It is not a little thing to have been baptized into the name of the Father, and of the Son, and of the Holy Ghost. It has made the area of your life not as small as you might want it to be, but as large as God intended it.

Now—our life is large

THE LORD'S SUPPER

TEXT: *1 Corinthians 11:23-26*
This is My Body . . . This is My Blood.

WHEN THE APOSTLE PAUL designated the time at which the Lord's Supper had been instituted he said, "On the night in which he was betrayed." He could have identified that night in many different ways. He might have said, "On the night in which Jesus washed the disciples' feet," "On the night in which Peter denied Him," "On the night in which Jesus was arrested." There were many things that happened that night. But he chose to say, "On the night in which Jesus was betrayed."

It is likely that he intended we should understand the meaning of this gracious act of Christ against the background of the betrayal. The dark treachery of Judas, who was willing to barter away his Master for the price of a slave, provides the proper background against which to view the gracious act of God's self-giving love. "This is my body, given for you; . . . this is my blood shed for you." If you follow the story as it is recorded in John's Gospel, you learn that Jesus identified the betrayer as the one to whom He gave the morsel of bread which had been dipped into His cup. In the custom of His time, to dip together into the same cup was a symbol and pledge of friendship and fellowship. And Judas, having dipped with Him in the cup, went out to betray Him.

168

As we celebrate the Lord's Supper we remember that night, for it helps us to understand how great is our need of Him, and how great is His love for us. But we do not just remember it as an event that happened. We remember Christ, who suffered, died, and rose again. "Do this in remembrance of me," He said. When we remember an event, we have to reach back across the days and years for it. We may be able to recall what it was that happened and how it all happened, but it does not happen over again. We have it with us only as a recollection. And when we remember a person, perhaps one who is no longer with us, then it is something more than just a recollection, is it not? There is something of that fellowship which we had with him which lives again. At least we may have the sense that he is somewhere in the balcony, among the great cloud of witnesses by which we are surrounded.

But when the one whom we remember is Christ, the eternal Son of God, then we have opened the door to His living presence here and now. You cannot imprison Him in that event that took place in an upper room in Jerusalem almost two thousand years ago. He is living; He is our "eternal contemporary." To remember Him is to let Him into our minds and hearts and affection in such a manner that we have real fellowship with Him here and now. So, as we take the cup and the bread, and re-enact in a sense the Supper in which our Lord was himself the host and in which He offered himself to them, He is as truly offering himself to us now. He is the Giver and the Gift again.

Or, look at it in another way. We have a saying that "The gift without the giver is bare." This is at least sometimes true. But when does a gift include the giver? You take a quantity of gold and alloy and fashion it into a ring. It is the same kind of material that could be shaped into many different products. And then you take such a ring and place it on the

169

finger of another. It may be only another bit of jewelry, perhaps expensive enough to be insured. But if a lover places the ring on the finger of his beloved, before God's altar and in the context of the marriage rite, it is not any longer just a ring, for with it two people have given themselves to one another, "in prosperity and in adversity, in sickness and in health," "until death do us part." Of course, there are no human analogies to what happens when God gives himself to men. Even in marriage we cannot give ourselves completely, for we are incurably selfish. But it is something like that—higher and purer as God's love is higher and purer than ours—which happens with these earthly means of bread and wine when they are offered to us by Christ who loved us and gave himself up for us, offered with the promise and blessing upon them. They become the bearers of His real Presence—His body and His blood.

When one forgives another a grievous fault, what is it that he is giving? Surely it is not merely words. Is he not offering himself in fellowship with the guilty? Far above any parallel, either in the extent of the offense or in the quality of the forgiveness, Christ gives himself with His pardon in the Supper.

We should think of the Lord's Supper, too, as a sort of a victory celebration. It is a foretaste of the Great Supper in heaven. Paul tells us that as often as we eat this bread and drink this cup we "proclaim the Lord's death until he comes." We are reminded that He who died rose again, and ascended to God's right hand, from whence He shall come to judge the living and the dead. The final word belongs to Him. We await the return of the King. And while we wait for that final triumph, we must be about His business. He will subdue all things under His feet; every knee will bow before Him, and every tongue will confess that He is Lord. We follow in the train of a Conqueror, and we are part of the conquering hosts. We are the instruments of His gracious will for the subduing of a sinful world. Indeed we, too, are His body, in and through whom He is now at work in the world.

G. K. Chesterton has somewhere reminded us of a practice in the medieval period among a company of Christian knights, who as they set out for battle received the Sacrament with one foot in the stirrup and then went forth to war. It is like that we take it—and then go out to do battle for the King and to triumph in His name.